Short Sentences
Long Remembered

Reading the Bible as Literature

Short Sentences Long Remembered

A GUIDED STUDY OF PROVERBS
AND OTHER WISDOM LITERATURE

LELAND RYKEN

LEXHAM PRESS

Short Sentences Long Remembered: A Guided Study of Proverbs and Other Wisdom Literature
© 2016 by Leland Ryken

Lexham Press, 1313 Commercial St., Bellingham, WA 98225
LexhamPress.com

First edition by Weaver Book Company.

Verse numbers appear in some Scripture quotations when the author refers to or comments on specific verses.

Print ISBN 9781683591603
Digital ISBN 9781683591610

Cover design and interior layout: Frank Gutbrod

Contents

Series Preface

This series is part of the mission of the publisher to equip Christians to understand and teach the Bible effectively by giving them reliable tools for handling the biblical text. Within that landscape, the niche that my volumes are designed to fill is the literary approach to the Bible. This has been my scholarly passion for nearly half a century. It is my belief that a literary approach to the Bible is the common reader's friend, in contrast to more specialized types of scholarship on the Bible.

Nonetheless, the literary approach to the Bible needs to be defended against legitimate fears by evangelical Christians, and through the years I have not scorned to clear the territory of misconceptions as part of my defense of a literary analysis of the Bible. In kernel form, my message has been this:

1. To view the Bible as literature is not a suspect modern idea, nor does it need to imply theological liberalism. The idea of the Bible as literature began with the writers of the Bible, who display literary qualities in their writings and who refer with technical precision to a wide range of literary genres such as psalm, proverb, parable, apocalypse, and many more.

2. Although fiction is a common trait of literature, it is not an essential feature of it. A work of literature can be replete with literary technique and artifice while remaining historically factual.

3. To approach the Bible as literature need not be characterized by viewing the Bible *only* as literature, any more than reading it as history requires us to see only the history of the Bible.

4. When we see literary qualities in the Bible we are not attempting to bring the Bible down to the level of ordinary literature; it is simply an objective statement about the inherent nature of the Bible. The Bible can be trusted to reveal its extraordinary qualities if we approach it with ordinary methods of literary analysis.

5. To sum up, it would be tragic if we allowed ourselves to be deprived of literary methods of analyzing the Bible by claims that are fallacies.

What, then, does it mean to approach the Bible as literature? A literary study of the Bible should begin where any other approach begins—by accepting as true all that the biblical writers claim about their book. These claims include its inspiration and superintendence by God, its infallibility, its historical truthfulness, its unique power to infiltrate people's lives, and its supreme authority.

With that as a foundation, a literary approach to the Bible is characterized by the following traits:

1. A literary approach acknowledges that the Bible comes to us in a predominantly literary format. In the words of C. S. Lewis, "There is a . . . sense in which the Bible, since it is after all literature, cannot properly be read except as literature; and the different parts of it as the different sorts

of literature they are."[1] The overall format of the Bible is that of an anthology of literature.

2. In keeping with that, a literary approach identifies the genres and other literary forms of the Bible and analyzes individual texts in keeping with those forms. An awareness of literary genres and forms programs how we analyze a biblical text and opens doors into a text that would otherwise remain closed.

3. A literary approach begins with the premise that a work of literature embodies universal human experience. Such truthfulness to human experience is complementary to the tendency of traditional approaches to the Bible to mainly see ideas in it. A literary approach corrects a commonly held fallacy that the Bible is a theology book with proof texts attached.

4. A literary approach to the Bible is ready to grant value to the biblical authors' skill with language and literary technique, seeing these as an added avenue to our enjoyment of the Bible.

5. A literary approach to the Bible takes its humble place alongside the two other main approaches—the theological and the historical. These three domains are established by the biblical writers themselves, who usually combine all three elements in their writings. However, in terms of space, the Bible is a predominantly literary book. Usually the historical and theological material is packaged in literary form.

These traits and methods of literary analysis govern the content of my series of guided studies to the genres of the Bible.

Although individual books in my series are organized by the leading literary genres that appear in the Bible, I need to highlight

---

1   *Reflections on the Psalms* (New York: Harcourt, Brace & World, 1958), 3.

that all of these genres have certain traits in common. Literature itself, en masse, makes up a homogenous whole. In fact, we can speak of *literature as a genre* (the title of the opening chapter of a book titled *Kinds of Literature*).[2] The traits that make up literature as a genre will simply be assumed in the volumes in this series. They include the following: universal, recognizable human experience concretely embodied as the subject matter; the packaging of this subject matter in distinctly literary genres; the authors' use of special resources of language that set their writing apart from everyday expository discourse; and stylistic excellence and other forms of artistry that are part of the beauty of a work of literature.

What are the advantages that come from applying the methods of literary analysis? In brief, they are as follows: an improved method of interacting with biblical texts in terms of the type of writing that they are; doing justice to the specificity of texts (again because the approach is tailored to the genres of a text); ability to see unifying patterns in a text; relating texts to everyday human experience; and enjoyment of the artistic skill of biblical authors.

Summary

A book needs to be read in keeping with its author's intention. We can see from the Bible itself that it is a thoroughly literary book. God superintended its authors to write a very (though not wholly) literary book. To pay adequate attention to the literary qualities of the Bible not only helps to unlock the meanings of the Bible; it is also a way of honoring the literary intentions of its authors. Surely biblical authors regarded everything that they put into their writing as important. We also need to regard those things as important.

---

2   Alastair Fowler, *Kinds of Literature: An Introduction to the Theory of Genres and Modes* (Oxford: Oxford University Press, 1985).

Introduction

How Wisdom Literature Edifies

This introductory chapter states broad generalizations about the content of wisdom literature and the ways in which that content can edify us. The remaining chapters explore the literary forms that make up wisdom literature. As those chapters unfold, it will be important not to lose sight of the content and edification that wisdom literature is designed to give us. Grasping the literary forms provides the means for interacting with the text itself, but that is a means to a further end. This introductory chapter is designed to provide avenues toward appropriating the truth and edification of wisdom literature. I would encourage readers to come back to the introduction from time to time so as to keep the edification in view.

Who Were the Wise Men Who Composed Wisdom Literature?

Our quest to master the wisdom literature of the Bible needs to begin with a look at the authors. In Old Testament times, the nation of believers recognized three categories of religious leaders —priests, prophets, and wise men. Jeremiah 18:18 helpfully names all three and hints at their respective roles: "the law shall not perish from the priest, nor counsel from the wise, nor the word from the prophet." (Ezekiel 7:26 uses the same formula, except that "the wise" are there called "elders.") The division of duties among these religious leaders was approximately as follows: the priests represented the people to God; the prophets brought God's word to people; the wise men taught their fellow humans. A formula that English poet William Wordsworth used for the poet fits the wise man perfectly: he is "a man speaking to men."

Two traits immediately emerge from this role of spokesman to people. One is that the wise men excelled in the ability to observe human character and life. The wise men were gifted observers of the human scene. They did not come to their listeners and readers with the oracular authority of the prophets, who prefaced their messages with "thus says the LORD." Instead, they authenticated their message with an appeal to shared human experience.

But the wise men did more than observe. They also taught. To some extent, the wisdom literature that this guide explores was the equivalent of our classroom instruction. Jeremiah 18:18 and Ezekiel 7:26 both attribute "counsel" to the wise men.

We need to assign one more primary trait to the wise men: in addition to being observers of the human scene and teachers of wisdom, they were wordsmiths. The chief evidence is the proverbs and aphorisms in which they enshrined their observations and instruction. Their "sayings" (a biblical synonym for "proverbs") sparkle with verbal artistry. They had a way with words that few achieve.

The writer of Ecclesiastes paints a self-portrait near the end of his collection of proverbs, and it is the best possible summary of the wise man and his place in society: "Besides being wise, the Preacher also taught the people knowledge, weighing and studying and arranging many proverbs with great care. The Preacher sought to find words of delight, and uprightly he wrote words of truth" (Eccl. 12:9–10).

What Is Wisdom?

In raising this question, I have in view specifically the view of wisdom that prevails in the wisdom literature of the Bible. No single definition will suffice as an answer to the question of what wisdom literature is. Instead, I offer angles of vision as gleaned from reliable sources.

Wisdom is *skill for living*. This implies that wisdom focuses on practical daily living and ties into the authors' task of observing life and human experience as noted above. The book of Proverbs contains observations and advice on such far-flung topics as farming, lawsuits, table manners, money management, avoiding bad companions, choosing a wife, and the delights of having grandchildren. This is not to minimize that other proverbs deal with the spiritual life—fearing God, worshiping properly, and enduring trial. Even here, though, the goal of the wise men is that people will navigate life well rather than poorly—with skill for living, in other words.

Closely aligned to that is a label that someone applied to the epistle of James: *faith that works*. Implicit in that formula is the idea that the wise men encourage people to *act* on the basis of their beliefs. This emphasis is not limited to the book of James. Jesus' Sermon on the Mount, for example, is a continuous stream of instruction about what Christians need to *do* and to *avoid*—action, in other words, in addition to belief. A famous biblical scholar used the formula "experiential knowledge" for this quality of wisdom.

Additionally, a lot will fall into place as we read wisdom literature if we are aware that this body of literature is devoted to the related topics of *human conduct* and *character formation*. The wise men are concerned with how people behave or act. But people act in accord with their inner character. We should therefore not view the emphasis on human action as urging people to externally obey a code of conduct. By commanding people to act according to their guidelines, the wise men actually want people to become righteous people.

What Is Aphoristic Thinking?

The adjective "aphoristic" is based on the noun "aphorism." An aphorism is a proverb—a concise, memorable statement of truth. To produce proverbs requires a special kind of thinking. This thinking starts with the writers of proverbs, but people who then assimilate and perpetuate proverbs by reading, memorizing, and reciting them in real-life situations are also engaging in aphoristic thinking.

One way to understand aphoristic thinking is that it is *a quest for order*. Life itself is a chaos of individual moments, experiences, and sensations. We have an urge to bring order to this chaos. Aphoristic thinking enables us to master the complexity of life by bringing human experience under the control of an observation that explains it. It does so by observing general principles that organize the repeatable situations of life. If this is true, then aphoristic thinking also expresses *an urge for understanding*. We are not content simply to experience things; we also want to understand them. A proverb expresses such understanding.

Aphoristic thinking is also *a quest for permanence*. It is not enough to express an insight and then lose it. Aphoristic thinking seeks to make the insight memorable. If it lives in our memory, it becomes permanent.

What Is the "Big Story," or Metanarrative, of Wisdom Literature?

Wisdom literature is made up of so many tiny units that it may seem to lack unity, but there is an overarching story that organizes the mass of details. If we simply start reading the book of

Proverbs, we will quickly sense that a great conflict is going on in the world. We are constantly confronted with statements that tell us to do *A* rather than *B* (portrayed as the opposite of *A*). The climax of Jesus' Sermon on the Mount is an apt summary of this dualistic view of life, with its contrasting picture of the wise man who builds his house on a rock and a foolish man who builds his house on the sand (Matt. 7:24–27).

The great spiritual battle between good and evil produces a related motif, namely, the necessity of choice. We might think of wisdom literature as the drama of the soul's choice (a phrase Dorothy L. Sayers used for Dante's *Inferno*). Even if a proverb is stated as an objective observation, the overall force of wisdom literature is that we understand that we are being confronted with a choice that is unavoidable. "The wage of the righteous leads to life, / the gain of the wicked to sin" (Prov. 10:16). The choice is ours. This motif of choice is well summarized by a passage near the end of Jesus' Sermon on the Mount, in which Jesus confronts his listeners with the need to choose between the broad way that leads to destruction and the narrow way that leads to life (Matt. 7:13–14).

How Did the Wise Men Disseminate Their Wisdom?

The social context of wisdom literature is complex and somewhat speculative. For starters, biblical scholars tell us that wisdom was an international phenomenon during the era of the Old Testament wise men. That is not hard to believe, inasmuch as other literary forms cultivated in Bible times show many parallels to those found in surrounding cultures.

Ancient cultures were oral cultures, so it is safe to assume that proverbial wisdom circulated orally as well as in written form. Of course, the wisdom literature of the Bible comes to us in written form. In turn, though, proverbs that we learn from a literary anthology receive their finest moment when they are uttered orally in the everyday situations where they apply. So one of the paradoxes of proverbial literature is that it is both oral and written.

Another paradox greets us when we ask where wisdom literature was originally taught. Experts in ancient history believe that Old Testament wisdom literature (especially the book of Proverbs) was taught in a courtly setting. On this view, the "son" who is repeatedly addressed in the book of Proverbs is specifically one of the aristocratic young men who were destined to become leaders in society. But the proverb is a form of folk literature. It arises from the common life, and its very simplicity implies a folk quality. According to Bible commentaries, Proverbs 1:20–21 paints a picture of how wise men taught—"aloud in the street," "in the markets," "at the head of the noisy streets," and "at the entrance of the city gates."

My own conclusion is that Old Testament wisdom in its original context was both a folk phenomenon and a courtly phenomenon. There are as many references to nature and rural living in Old Testament wisdom as to kings. Most of the proverbs are universal and apply to every person.

The foregoing discussion covers wisdom literature in its original context. That is a useful piece of information, but for us, wisdom literature is a written text just like the rest of the Bible. To understand it, we need to apply the ordinary rules of literary analysis. The only imprint of the original teaching situation is that wisdom literature is more directly didactic ("having the intention to teach") than the stories and poems of the Bible are, which operate with a certain indirectness.

What Is Wisdom Literature?

The question of how teachers of any type disseminate their instruction leaves unanswered the question of how the materials of their teaching arose in the first place. Teachers pass on inherited material. If we picture an ancient teacher standing before a class of aristocratic young people or a street teacher addressing the masses, in both cases we should not picture the teacher as composing his own material on the spot. A teacher today teaches from a textbook. The wisdom books of the Bible are the equivalent of a textbook.

So who composed the wisdom books? They were authors who flaunted their literary skill in virtually every line that they composed. As later chapters in this guide explore the literary forms of wisdom literature, we will find it hard to picture a teacher at all. What will grab our attention is the literary expertise of the authors who composed the proverbs and collected them in anthologies. I tell my classes that the task of a literary author is threefold—to observe and record human experience, to interpret the experiences that are portrayed, and to entertain us with literary form and technique. The proverbs that make up wisdom literature perform exactly those three functions.

Where Do We Find Wisdom Literature in the Bible?

This question is not as easily answered as we might think. If we begin with the individual proverb as the essential form of wisdom, we need to conclude that wisdom literature appears on virtually every page of the Bible. The Bible is the most aphoristic book of the Western world. I have not cast my net as widely as the individual proverbs that permeate the Bible, but what I say about the proverb as a literary form does apply to those proverbs.

In this guide, I take all of my data from four undisputed texts of wisdom literature. They are the Old Testament books of Proverbs and Ecclesiastes, the epistle of James, and Jesus' Sermon on the Mount. The latter leads to the following thoughts about Jesus as wise man, teacher, or rabbi.

The sayings of Jesus are scattered throughout the Gospels. It would have been defensible to include all of those sayings in my analysis. But the designation "wisdom literature" implies a whole book or discourse—an extensive and unified composition. The Sermon on the Mount possesses all of the typical traits of a wisdom literature text.

General Traits of a Proverb

The primary (but not only) literary form of wisdom literature is the proverb. In the Bible, the proverb is also known by synonyms, the most common of which is "saying." The inscription to the book of Proverbs teases us into seeing even more in a proverb or saying by listing "words" and "riddles" as variants. Additionally, a concise memorable saying is known by the label "aphorism," and I myself often use the adjective "aphoristic" in my teaching of literature. The Bible is an aphoristic book. Yet another synonym for proverb is "epigram."

The opening chapters of this guide focus specifically on the proverb as a literary form—first its general traits and then specific techniques used by writers of the wisdom books and texts.

Obstacles to Properly Valuing the Proverb as a Literary Form

One of the changes I can chart over the course of my career in the Bible as literature is a growing appreciation for the proverb as literary genre. Implicit in that statement is that I began with an undervaluing of proverbs as a form of literature. I want to reach back to my earlier years and start with a discussion of the obstacles that stand in the way of giving biblical proverbs their due. The goal is to clear the path of roadblocks. I will delineate five obstacles, and I need to signal from the start that I am not listing them because I think they are the last word but because we need to understand the problem before we can find solutions.

1. *A shift in cultural sensibility.* Certain cultures are oriented toward proverbs and aphoristic thinking. Ancient cultures were proverbial cultures. Much of their knowledge and wisdom was preserved and passed on in the form of proverbs. One reason for this is that they were oral cultures rather than print cultures, and oral cultures depend on forms of speech that can be remembered and disseminated.

   The modern age is not an oral age and is not oriented toward proverbial knowledge. Having said that, I need to add that even if modern culture as a whole is not given to aphoristic thinking, groups and individuals within it are. My mother was a walking encyclopedia of proverbs, and my life was much enriched by her ability to pronounce a proverb in the real-life situation where it applied.

   Overall, though, we live in an age that does not think easily in terms of proverbs. Proverbs thrive in cultures that have a certain sensibility of thought and speech, and our society does not meet that criterion. It is not just a matter of not valuing proverbs; it is also a matter of lacking the mental equipment to cultivate them as a literary form. An advertising slogan is not a proverb.

2. *Loss of memorizing.* The reason oral cultures developed such forms as proverbs and the verse form of parallelism is that these are mnemonic devices (aids to memory). By contrast, we are a print and digital culture. Only a small segment of contemporary society memorizes in the old sense. Merely reading a succession of proverbs is of very limited appeal or

usefulness. The true context for a proverb is not a collection or anthology of proverbs but actual situations of life. For a proverb to rise to our lips on such occasions, we need to be able to call the proverb to mind. Our cultural situation makes that difficult.

3. *Indifference to wisdom.* There is a sense in which proverbs were the ancient version of information storage and retrieval. I use that terminology to highlight the function served by proverbs. But the word "information" comes from our own age and is incorrect when applied to proverbs. Proverbs do not convey information; they convey wisdom. By contrast, we live in the information age. As far back as 1936, T. S. Eliot wrote, "Where is the wisdom we have lost in knowledge? / Where is the knowledge we have lost in information?"

   So wisdom starts with a strike against it: whereas "wisdom" and "folly" were dominant concepts in Bible times (as seen in the frequency with which those words appear in wisdom literature), in the modern age we have no clear understanding of what wisdom is. Before we can relish the proverb as a literary form, we need to understand what wisdom is because the proverb is the natural vehicle for expressing wisdom.

4. *The disparagement of proverbs by biblical scholars.* When I see the condescending attitude that some biblical scholars display toward the proverb, it is no wonder that the rank-and-file Christian does not value it. A well-known book on the genres of the Bible calls proverbs "catchy little couplets." Who is likely to summon enthusiasm for catchy little couplets? Other familiar sources assert that biblical proverbs "do not reflect moral laws that are to be applied absolutely," and that "proverbs are worded to be memorable, not technically precise."

   There are, indeed, interpretive guidelines and cautions that need to be stated, but these are not the first or only things we should say about the proverb as a literary form. It is a qualifier that we should add at the end of the discussion to prevent possible misinterpretation; the first thing to assert with conviction is that proverbs express truth.

5. *The brevity of the form.* The strength of the proverb is its conciseness. It expresses truth with a punch. But that is also a limitation. Literature is something we read and analyze and teach. What can be done with a concise proverb in these contexts? It is a problem that we need to solve. A common subtype in the proverbial literature of the Bible is proverb clusters, and these can be treated as we do other familiar forms such as a lyric poem or a meditation on a subject. But many of the proverbs appear in lists of individual proverbs, each on a different subject. Such a passage poses genuine problems for devotional reading and teaching.

There are ways to surmount the obstacles I have delineated, and these will occupy the rest of this guide. For the remainder of this chapter, I explore the general traits of the proverb as a literary form. I would not say that these traits offer solutions to the problems I have delineated, but they give us the right expectations. If we understand the defining traits of a proverb, we have some preliminary ways of analyzing a proverb.

Proverbs Are Apt and Memorable

When we first hear or read a proverb, we obviously do not know whether we will remember it, but we sense that it has a striking effect on us, and we know that it is *worthy* of memory. "An excellent wife is the crown of her husband" (Prov. 12:4). "Whatever your hand finds to do, do it with your might" (Eccl. 9:10). "Be doers of the word, and not hearers only" (James 1:22). Not all proverbs are that easy to remember, but the general tendency of proverbs is to stick in our minds.

It is the aim of a proverb to make an insight permanent. I have benefited from the following commentary on the nature of a proverb: "to epigrammatize an experience is to strip it down, to cut away irrelevance, to eliminate local, specific, and descriptive detail, to reduce it to and fix it in its most permanent and stable aspect."[3] A proverb fixes an insight or observation on human experience in its permanent and stable aspect.

Some proverbs pack such a punch that they not only express an insight but also compel it. I would certainly not raise the bar that high for all proverbs, but it is true of many proverbs. The most striking example of this in my own experience comes from beyond the Bible. Having been to England many times, things suddenly fell into place for me when I read the following aphorism: "The British will not change anything they can endure; Americans will not endure anything they can change." An example from the Bible is Proverbs 10:7: "The memory of the righteous is a blessing." Some proverbs have this quality of being a flash of insight.

Proverbs share with literature generally an ability to overcome the cliché effect of ordinary discourse. They often possess arresting strangeness. They do not strike us as everyday discourse but as language on display. To create an aphorism requires two things at least: an extraordinary power of observation or insight and a skill with language that most people lack. It is a literary gift.

What methodology for analyzing a proverb emerges from the foregoing? I have found that asking what it is in a given proverb that makes it striking or arresting yields preliminary insight into its meaning. I have learned to ask, What makes this proverb apt and memorable?

---

3   Barbara Herrnstein Smith, *Poetic Closure: A Study of How Poems End* (Chicago: University of Chicago Press, 1968), 208.

> ## LEARNING BY DOING
>
> The starting point for performing this exercise is to review the concepts that have been stated in preceding paragraphs. Then see how that feeds into your experience of the following proverbs. Do not do this hastily; ponder each proverb in light of the principles that have been stated.
>
> - "The fear of the LORD is the beginning of knowledge" (Prov. 1:7).
> - "Better is a dry morsel with quiet / than a house full of feasting with strife" (Prov. 17:1).
> - "There is nothing new under the sun" (Eccl. 1:9).
> - "No one can serve two masters" (Matt. 6:24).
> - "For as the body apart from the spirit is dead, so also faith apart from works is dead" (James 2:26).

Proverbs Are Simple

One of the paradoxes of proverbs is that they are both simple and complex. I decided to devote separate modules to each of these qualities so each will stand out.

Proverbs are short and simple at the surface level, though of course there is variability of length. The proverbs listed immediately above are succinct. Nonetheless, if we start browsing the wisdom books, we often find proverbs that keep expanding until the initial statement has become four or five lines or more. Here is an example (Prov. 24:19–20):

> Fret not yourself because of evildoers,
> > and be not envious of the wicked,
> for the evil man has no future;
> > the lamp of the wicked will be put out.

This is a more complex construction than the simple one-liner. It takes more effort to memorize it. But the individual sentence elements are simple. The complexity arises from the parallelism in which each half of the command-plus-reason is repeated, forming two pairs of lines.

The simplicity of a proverb springs from one of its purposes, namely, to strip an experience down to its core. A proverb is an insight into the repeatable situations of life. This requires a universal principle rather than specific examples. In turn, a universal is simple.

The result of this simplicity is that anyone can grasp a proverb once it is understood. Even when ancient proverbial literature was taught to aristocratic youth at court, paradoxically proverbs are also a form of folk literature. It doesn't take a college education to understand that "grandchildren are the crown of the aged" (Prov. 17:6) or that "every healthy tree bears good fruit" (Matt. 7:17).

What interpretive action does the simplicity of a proverb require of us? First, we can profitably analyze what makes a given proverb simple. Second, we can relish and enjoy that simplicity. There is much in the Bible that is mysterious and difficult. Comparatively speaking, proverbs allow us to take a relaxing break.

LEARNING BY DOING

Here are three simple proverbs that will enable you to apply the foregoing:

- "Light is sweet, and it is pleasant for the eyes to see the sun" (Eccl. 11:7).
- "Let another praise you, and not your own mouth" (Prov. 27:2).
- "If we put bits into the mouths of horses so that they obey us, we guide their whole bodies as well" (James 3:3).

Proverbs Are Complex and Profound

Can proverbs be both simple and complex? Yes. While proverbs are simple, they are also complex and profound in multiple ways. I explore their complexity first. I need to begin by acknowledging that there is a range of simplicity and complexity. Some proverbs are of the type discussed in the preceding module, and some are mysterious and elusive. In fact, in the inscription to the book of Proverbs, the author uses the word "riddle" as a synonym for "proverb" (1:6). I take this up in detail later in this guide. The following proverb falls in the middle of the continuum of simplicity-complexity: "He who loves money will not be satisfied with money" (Eccl. 5:10). On one level, this is a simple proverb. The complexity emerges when we ponder *why* the person who loves money will never be satisfied with it. There are at least two reasons: (1) money does not satisfy permanently and at the deepest level, so of course a person is not content with money; (2) the appetite for money grows by indulgence and is therefore insatiable.

There is a second type of complexity as well, having to do with the application of a proverb. A proverb must be put into real-life situations where it applies. When we do that, we find that we never get to the end of the application. That represents complexity. To take the financial proverb quoted in the preceding paragraph, we keep seeing examples of the truth in our lives and in the lives of people around us.

If proverbs are sometimes complex in the ways just noted, they are also profound. In contrast to a bumper-sticker slogan, biblical proverbs deal with the serious and profound issues of life. Although a few of them are observations about everyday life such as anyone might make, they usually deal with serious moral and spiritual principles. Here is an example: "Whoever conceals his transgressions will not prosper, / but he who confesses and forsakes them will obtain mercy" (Prov. 28:13).

What interpretive methods do the complexity and profundity of a proverb require? They require that we spend the amount of time and mental energy required to see the dimensions that I have discussed above. There is an observation level to proverbs, but often also an analytic and interpretive level. Application to real-life situations certainly requires us to reflect on the implications of a proverb.

LEARNING BY DOING

The following proverbs provide scope for analyzing the complexity and profundity of proverbs:

- "The path of the righteous is like the light of dawn, / which shines brighter and brighter until full day" (Prov. 4:18).
- "Remember also your Creator in the days of your youth, before the evil days come and the years draw near of which you will say, 'I have no pleasure in them'" (Eccl. 12:1).
- "Blessed are those who mourn, for they shall be comforted" (Matt. 5:4).
- "Humble yourselves before the Lord, and he will exalt you" (James 4:10).

Proverbs Are Simultaneously Specific and General or Universal

Proverbs combine the particular with the universal. This will require our best thinking. In one category are proverbs that are filled with concrete images and situations. "Like cold water to a thirsty soul, / so is good news from a far country" (Prov. 25:25). "A whip for the horse, a bridle for the donkey, / and a rod for the back of fools" (Prov. 26:3).

But there are also proverbs that operate at a greater level of generalization, in contrast to those that give us concrete images. "A wise man is full of strength, / and a man of knowledge enhances his might" (Prov. 24:5). The vocabulary in that proverb is abstract. So even at the surface level, proverbs as an aggregate intermingle the specific and the general.

But there is more to the picture than this. Proverbs always express an observation about a general tendency of life, not a unique occurrence. Even when a proverb gives us a particular situation, we understand that this particular situation is representative of the human situation more generally. An example is the following proverb: "My son, if your heart is wise, / my heart too will be glad" (Prov. 23:15). That is not only about one son but also about every wise son who pleases his father. In other words, it extends universally.

Then there is a whole different category of proverbs that are really metaphoric, even though the terminology is specific. An example is Ecclesiastes 10:18: "Through sloth the roof sinks in, / and through indolence the house leaks." There is a physical level of truth here, inasmuch as people who do not keep their roof in good repair sooner or later experience leaks. But there is a metaphoric level as well. As a teacher, I see metaphoric roofs that leak as a result of sloth every semester.

What are the interpretive implications? We need to have our antennae up for the intermingling of specific and general, noting each where it appears. Concrete language and pictures are "right-brain discourse" and need to be experienced as such. When the concrete pictures are metaphoric as well as literal, we need to identify the metaphoric level. In all instances, we need to be attuned to the fact that a proverb deals with universal, repeatable situations, not once-only ones.

LEARNING BY DOING

The foregoing material is difficult to grasp. You can profitably begin this exercise by reviewing it. Then apply the material to the following proverbs:

- "The wise lay up knowledge, / but the mouth of a fool brings ruin near" (Prov. 10:14).
- "Whoever who works his land will have plenty of bread, / but he who follows worthless pursuits will have plenty of poverty" (Prov. 28:19).
- "All are from the dust, and to dust all return" (Eccl. 3:20).
- "A harvest of righteousness is sown in peace by those who make peace" (James 3:18).

The Proverb at Its Core

In our exploration of the proverb as a literary form, we need to start at the micro level. The basic building block of proverbial literature is such minutiae as poetic images, figures of speech, one-sentence units, and various types of parallelism. It makes sense to start at the level of building blocks.

The One-Sentence and Two-Line Proverb

To my surprise, as I delved into the proverb for purposes of this guide, I discovered that the only good starting point is syntax, or sentence structure. The basic unit of a biblical proverb is the single sentence. The simplest form of proverb, found in prose but rarely in biblical poetry, is what is grammatically called a simple sentence with a single independent (freestanding) clause (in contrast to a compound sentence with two independent clauses). Here is an example of a simple one-sentence proverb: "a threefold cord is not quickly broken" (Eccl. 4:12). It turns out that very few biblical proverbs are this simple; most include additional phrases or clauses.

When a proverb is expressed in the form of poetry, the one-sentence proverb automatically becomes a two-line proverb, even though it is still a single sentence. This is because of the verse form of parallelism, which stipulates that material be packaged in two-line units. The following are examples of one-sentence, two-line proverbs:

- "Righteousness exalts a nation,
  but sin is a reproach to any people" (Prov. 14:34).
- "The eyes of the LORD are in every place,
  keeping watch on the evil and the good" (Prov. 15:3).
- "The getting of treasures by a lying tongue
  is a fleeting vapor and a snare of death" (Prov. 21:6).

These are one-sentence proverbs that are also two-line units. If the second and third examples appeared in prose, they would be a single line, but the poetic format requires that they appear as two lines.

I note as a point of information that the impulse toward balancing one sentence element with a second one is so much a part of the deep structure of biblical thinking that it exerts a strong pressure even in prose. We continuously encounter statements in which the initial shoe falls and then we wait for the second one to fall, as in these examples:

- "For my yoke is easy, and my burden is light" (Matt. 11:30).
- "Two are better than one, because they have a good reward for their toil" (Eccl. 4:9).
- "Draw near to God, and he will draw near to you" (James 4:8).

In the second example, the statement that "two are better than one" is an aphorism that could stand alone, but the rhythm of balance in the Bible is such that we expect something more to be added, as indeed it is.

The foregoing discussion does not yield a methodology for analysis. It simply calls attention to the format in which individual proverbs are expressed in the Bible. This is useful information for seeing what is before us.

A Primer on the Verse Form of Parallelism

We need to expand the foregoing discussion and get the larger picture before us. This larger picture consists of the verse form known as *parallelism*. The principle of organization that underlies parallelism is that of saying something twice in similar grammatical form but in different words and images. There is an element of sameness that is carried over from the first line to the second, and also an element of otherness that is added.

The various types of parallelism that make up the verse form of biblical poetry are a menu from which authors of proverbs select. The following three types of parallelism make up the menu, with each one accompanied by an example:

- *Synonymous parallelism,* in which the second line restates the same truth as the first in a similar way: "A false witness will not go unpunished, / and he who breathes out lies will not escape" (Prov. 19:5). Every major element of the first line has an "answering" element in the second line.
- *Antithetic parallelism,* in which the second line states the truth of the first line in a contrasting way: "The way of a fool is right in his own eyes, / but a wise man listens to advice" (Prov. 12:15).
- *Synthetic ("growing") parallelism,* in which the second line adds to the first line or completes it: "The fear of the LORD is a fountain of life, / that one may turn away from the snares of death" (Prov. 14:27).

Just for the record, there is a fourth type of parallelism that appears elsewhere in the Bible but not in a significant way in wisdom literature. It is known as *climactic parallelism,* in which the second line repeats part of the first line (which had stopped in the middle of a statement) and then completes it with a note of triumph. This type of parallelism apparently fit the purposes of poets writing praise psalms but not wise men composing proverbs.

Something further needs to be said about synthetic parallelism. Strictly speaking, nothing is parallel. The second line completes the thought that is introduced in the first line, but there are no parallel elements between the two lines. Why, then, is it called parallelism? The answer is that it is a two-line unit, just like other forms of parallelism. It therefore functions like the other forms in having two halves. It *feels* like parallelism, even though technically it does not meet the definition.

Does parallelism contribute to the meaning of a proverb, or is it a purely artistic component that adds beauty? I believe that it contributes to the meaning and needs to be analyzed and interpreted. In the case of synonymous parallelism, we should observe the words chosen as synonyms and analyze how the parallel word or image adds to our understanding as compared to what it would be like if we had only the one term. With antithetic parallelism, we can analyze how the contrasting words or images add to our understanding of the utterance, asking why a given element was chosen as the opposite of the other. With synthetic, or "growing," parallelism, we can ponder how the second line adds to our understanding beyond the first line by itself, and we can theorize about why the author chose this particular "add-on" when other alternatives existed.

I want to return to the point about the aesthetics or beauty that the verse form of parallelism brings to a proverb. The proverbs are examples of verbal beauty. They are chiseled statements, built out of carefully chosen words, artfully arranged and capturing a high point of human insight. This element of artistic beauty and skillful handling of style is an added avenue to enjoying proverbs. It also partly explains why proverbs are memorable.

LEARNING BY DOING

The following list of proverbs will enable you to apply the material covered in the unit on parallelism; if necessary, consult the preceding discussion for "prompts."

- "He who gathers in summer is a prudent son, but he who sleeps in harvest is a son who brings shame" (Prov. 10:5).
- "Whoever walks with the wise becomes wise, but the companion of fools will suffer harm" (Prov. 13:20).
- "If a ruler listens to falsehood, all his officials will be wicked" (Prov. 29:12).
- "All the toil of man is for his mouth, yet his appetite is not satisfied" (Eccl. 6:7).
- "For the upright will inhabit the land, and those with integrity will remain in it" (Prov. 2:21).

Poetry

Half of the wisdom and proverbial literature in the Bible is prose, and half of it is poetry. The entire book of Proverbs is poetic, and some passages in Ecclesiastes are. The purpose of this module is to provide a refresher on the basics of poetry.

One dimension of poetry has already been covered, namely, the way in which poetry is embodied in the verse form of parallelism. With most biblical poetry, I am inclined to say that parallelism is merely the verse form in which the content is packaged, but the previous module has suggested that parallelism packs a bigger punch than normal in the proverbs of the Bible.

Nonetheless, the essence or most important aspect of poetry is that its content is expressed with imagery and figurative language. These elements make up the *poetic idiom,* also called *poetic texture.* To extract the truth of a poetic statement, we need to unpack the meanings of the poetic texture. For the remainder of this module, I list, define, and illustrate the leading figures of speech and delineate the rules of interpretation for each one.

Image and imagery. An image is any word naming a concrete thing or action. The word "imagery" is a virtual synonym for "image," but it is also used to refer to the aggregate of images in a passage or an image cluster that forms a motif (such as the imagery of the path in wisdom literature). The following passages are built out of images or imagery:

- "Where there are no oxen, the manger is clean,
  but abundant crops come by the strength of the ox"
  (Prov. 14:4).
- "Do not move an ancient landmark or enter the fields
  of the fatherless" (Prov. 23:10).
- "The sun rises, and the sun goes down, and hastens to
  the place where it rises" (Eccl. 1:5).

These are examples of "straight images," meaning that they are not metaphors or similes. This leads me to make two additional observations. First, it is relatively difficult to find examples of straight images in proverbial literature; most occurrences of imagery are part of figurative language, as in Proverbs 13:9: "The light of the righteous rejoices, / but the lamp of the wicked will be put out." Second, much of the imagery in proverbial literature is abstract rather than concrete. For example, "The righteous hates falsehood, / but the wicked brings shame and disgrace" (Prov. 13:5). The right term for words like "righteous," "falsehood," "wicked," "shame," and "disgrace" is "conceptual imagery." These words function just like concrete imagery, but they name abstractions.

Straight images require three interpretive actions:

- We need to experience the literal properties of the image as fully as possible, making sure that we know what the proverb wishes us to picture.
- We need to identify the connotations of the image, including emotional meanings.
- We need to analyze the logic of the image: why did the writer choose this image for this particular subject?

Metaphor and simile. A metaphor is an implied comparison in which *A* is said to be *B*. For example: "The name of the LORD is a strong tower" (Prov. 18:10). A simile also asserts a correspondence between two things, but it uses the explicit formula "like" or "as": "A king's wrath is like the growling of a lion" (Prov. 19:12). Except for the presence or absence of the "like" or "as," metaphor and simile are the same, being a form of analogy.

Our interpretive task with metaphor and simile is twofold:

- A metaphor or simile is an image first of all, before it becomes a comparison. We need to experience level A as fully as possible, along the lines of what was said above about the straight image.
- Then we need to carry over the meanings from level A to the actual subject of the statement (level B). The etymology of the word "metaphor" speaks volumes: it is based on two Greek words that mean "to carry over." Having experienced the literal properties of a strong tower, we need to *carry over* those meanings and associations to "the name of the LORD," meaning the person of God. Exactly *how* is God a strong tower?

Personification. Personification consists of treating some-thing nonhuman as though it were human by attributing human qualities to it. This technique dominates Proverbs 1–9, where the abstractions Wisdom and Folly are portrayed as imposing women who compete with each other to capture the allegiance of the young man to whom much of those chapters is addressed. But personification appears intermittently elsewhere:

- "The wisest of women builds her house, / but folly with her own hands tears it down" (Prov. 14:1). The abstraction folly does not possess hands capable of dismantling a house; it is personified as having that capability.
- "A fool's lips walk into a fight" (Prov. 18:6). Lips can't literally walk into a fight; they are portrayed as though they are a person.

The interpretive task is to identify a personification when we find one, not attempting to interpret the statement literally. Often we can relish the inventiveness of the author in producing a clever personification, and we can analyze what added meaning or impact the statement has as a result of the personification.

To sum up, half of the wisdom literature of the Bible is enshrined in poetry. We cannot deal correctly with these parts of the Bible without applying all the ordinary rules of poetic inter-pretation. To read poetic proverbs as straightforward expository prose is to reduce them to a superficial level.

Nonetheless, I want to introduce an unexpected final thought. Literary scholars acknowledge something called the "poetry of statement." Such poetry appears in a verse form (in the Bible, parallelism), so we recognize it as poetry, but it does not employ the resources of poetry such as imagery and figurative language. It carries its meaning on the surface the way everyday discourse does. For example: "Pride goes before destruction, / and a haughty spirit before a fall" (Prov. 16:18). Despite the *prevalence* of poetry in proverbial literature, we should avoid making the material more poetic than it is.

LEARNING BY DOING

The following passage (Prov. 20:10–17) is a typical specimen of what we find in the book of Proverbs; it will enable you to apply some of what was said in the preceding module.

Unequal weights and unequal measures
    are both alike an abomination to the LORD.
Even a child makes himself known by his acts,
    by whether his conduct is pure and upright.
The hearing ear and the seeing eye,
    the LORD has made them both.
Love not sleep, lest you come to poverty;
    open your eyes, and you will have plenty of bread.
"Bad, Bad," says the buyer,
    but when he goes away, then he boasts.
There is gold and abundance of costly stones,
    but the lips of knowledge are a precious jewel.
Take a man's garment when he has put up security for a
    stranger, and hold it in pledge when he puts up security
    for foreigners.
Bread gained by deceit is sweet to a man,
    but afterward his mouth will be full of gravel.

Observation and Command as the Two Primary Forms

Since this chapter is devoted to the proverb at its core, I want to take time to state something that is obvious if we are clued into it but easy to overlook if we are not. The individual proverbs fall into two basic categories, and it is useful to know this as we interact with a proverb.

Most proverbs are stated as an observation about life, as in the following example (Prov. 19:14): "House and wealth are inherited from fathers, / but a prudent wife is from the LORD." For reasons that will be noted in the following chapter on interpreting proverbs, the observational format is actually much the same in effect as a command. We assimilate the observation in such a way as to want to act in a good way or reject wrong behavior.

The other format is the command. Although most proverbs are observational, interspersed among the observations are occasional commands: "Listen to advice and accept instruction, / that you may gain wisdom in the future" (Prov. 19:20). In some of the late chapters of Proverbs, the command format becomes the dominant one, as in the following list (Prov. 23:9–10, 12–13):

> Do not speak in the hearing of a fool,
>> for he will despise the good sense of your words.
> Do not move an ancient landmark
>> or enter the fields of the fatherless . . .
> Apply your heart to instruction
>> and your ear to words of knowledge.
> Do not withhold discipline from a child;
>> if you strike him with a rod, he will not die.

Commands are also frequent in the first nine chapters of Proverbs, where the father extends many commands regarding what to do and what not to do.

Riddles

For most of my life, I was totally baffled by a detail in the inscription to the book of Proverbs. In Proverbs 1:6, the writer gives us four synonyms for the literary genres that will appear in the book that follows: "proverb," "saying," "words," and "riddles"—"words *of the wise and their riddles,*" in case we are skeptical that the author is talking about wisdom literature. What does a riddle have in common with a proverb or saying?

A riddle is a statement that initially perplexes us. It teases us into wondering what it means and requires us to figure that out. There is much in the book of Proverbs and other proverbial literature that requires "figuring out."

To start at the most indisputable level, there are obvious riddles in the book of Proverbs. The most famous occurs in 23:29–35. It starts out with questions the way a riddle does: Who has woe? Who has sorrow? / Who has strife? Who has complaining? And so forth. (I joke with my classes that it is a description of someone who has pulled an all-nighter.) After the vivid description, the passage itself tells us the answer to the riddle, namely, the drunkard. Proverbs 30:4 is phrased as a riddle:

> Who has ascended to heaven and come down?
>> Who has gathered the wind in his fists?
> Who has wrapped up the waters in a garment?
>> Who has established all the ends of the earth?
> What is his name, and what is his son's name?
>> Surely you know!

I would place the numerical proverbs that appear late in the book of Proverbs into the category of riddle. If we had only the following lead-in (Prov. 30:24), we would not have a clue as to what the "four things" are: "Four things on earth are small, / but they are exceedingly wise." Likewise the following lead-in (Prov. 30:29):

"Three things are stately in their tread; / four are stately in their stride." Which is it—three or four? As with any riddle, we don't know the answer unless we are "in" on the riddle.

But the inscription links riddles with proverbs, not with larger passages. Many proverbs in the Old Testament book of Proverbs are like riddles in constituting a mystery that needs to be solved. I delineate two categories of such proverbs.

The first category consists of mysterious proverbs that puzzle us in themselves. They lead us to ask, What does that mean? Below are five examples:

- "Whoever winks the eye causes trouble" (Prov. 10:10). How can winking an eye cause trouble?
- "The mercy of the wicked is cruel" (Prov. 12:10). How can mercy be cruel?
- "The ransom of a man's life is his wealth, / but a poor man hears no threat" (Prov. 13:8). We scratch our heads and wonder what this means.
- "Take a man's garment when he has put up security for a stranger, / and hold it in pledge when he puts up security for an adulteress" (Prov. 27:13). This is a proverb that sends me scurrying to the notes in a study Bible.
- "Cast your bread upon the waters, / for you will find it after many days" (Eccl. 11:1). Commentators do not agree among themselves as to what this means. (Just for the record, I accept the down-to-earth interpretation "diversify your investments.")

I have a simple rule of thumb for labeling a proverb a riddle: if I can't figure it out on my own and need to go a commentary or study Bible, it has the quality of a riddle.

The second category is proverbs whose meaning is clear but that leave us wondering why they are in the book of Proverbs or in the specific context where they appear. Here are examples:

- "One pretends to be rich, yet has nothing; / another pretends to be poor, yet has great wealth" (Prov. 13:7). True enough, but how does that observation help us toward godliness?
- "The glory of young men is their strength, / but the splendor of old men is their gray hair" (Prov. 20:29).
- "Whoever plans to do evil / will be called a schemer" (Prov. 24:8).
- "Whoever digs a pit will fall into it" (Prov. 26:27).

All of these observations are self-evident; our perplexity arises from wondering what the edification is.

We can draw several conclusions from the presence of such riddling. Being the product of the folk imagination, proverbs can lull us into thinking that they are uniformly simple and easily understood. The intermittent appearance of riddles jolts us into an awareness that proverbs require our best effort and should not be the occasion for us to take a holiday of the mind. I find additionally that the riddling aspect of proverbs makes proverbial literature more interesting and enjoyable. Finally, when I find myself unable to make sense of a proverb, I take comfort in knowing that it is in the nature of proverbs sometimes to be elusive and mysterious. I need not suffer a breakdown of self-esteem for needing to consult a reference book in order to make sense of a given proverb.

Widening the Scope

Antithesis, Comparison, Analogy, and Proverb Formulas

T he preceding chapter considered the proverb at its core, as it is in itself. This chapter is a follow-up. It widens the scope to something broader than the individual proverb with its simple syntax, parallelism, and poetic idiom. As with the preceding chapter, this one deals with *poetic* wisdom literature, since prose wisdom is more diffuse and follows a different dynamic.

Catalog of Wisdom Sayings

My first category is so obvious that separate mention of it might seem unnecessary, but here as elsewhere in life it is important not to overlook the obvious. The basic, foundational component in poetic wisdom literature is the list of proverbs. Even when a list forms a proverb cluster on a common topic, the cluster is built out of individual proverbs. Here is what a catalog of proverbs looks like (Prov. 13:1–2):

A wise son hears his father's instruction,
    but a scoffer does not listen to rebuke.
From the fruit of his mouth a man eats what is good,
    but the desire of the treacherous is for violence.

We need to draw certain conclusions about the catalog structure of poetic wisdom literature. First, a simple form like the catalog of proverbs shows the folk imagination at work. We can't get more elementary than a simple list. The repetitiousness of the catalog of proverbs brings with it a problem that we need to acknowledge and solve, namely, the monotony that sets in as we read one proverb after another. One solution is to alternate reading a passage of wisdom poetry with other types of material. Another is to read slowly and meditatively, pondering each proverb, analyzing it along the lines already suggested in the preceding chapters and as elaborated in coming chapters.

Antithesis

The previous chapter discussed antithetic parallelism as one of three types of parallelism that appears in wisdom literature. But the principle of conflict between opposites is much more deeply infused into wisdom literature than that. It is part of the deep structure of wisdom in the Bible, and this provides the context for what I am about to say. An early champion of the literary approach to the Bible said something that has stayed with me for nearly half a century, namely, that "antithesis is the very life blood of the proverb."

Simply to list antithetic parallelism as one of three options is to conceal the dominance of that form in poetic wisdom literature. The point that needs to be emphasized is that many passages in the book of Proverbs consist of strings of proverbs embodied in antithetic parallelism. Here is a specimen (Prov. 15:25–27):

The LORD tears down the house of the proud
    but maintains the widow's boundaries.
The thoughts of the wicked are an abomination to the LORD,
    but gracious words are pure.
Whoever is greedy for unjust gain troubles his own household,
    but he who hates bribes will live.

The first application is that we need to be aware of how much antithesis exists in poetic wisdom literature. We can profitably analyze what the effect is, and reflect on the worldview that emerges from the sharp cleavage between opposites that we find.

From lists of individual proverbs structured as a contrast we move to slightly larger units. The image of the path or way is a recurrent master image in biblical wisdom literature, and often it is turned into a conflict between good and bad pathways. The following passage (Prov. 2:10–13) is an excerpt from a larger passage that contrasts the way of wisdom and the way of evil:

for wisdom will come into your heart,
    and knowledge will be pleasant to your soul;
discretion will watch over you,
    understanding will guard you,
delivering you from the way of evil,
    from men of perverted speech,
who forsake the paths of uprightness
    to walk in the ways of darkness.

If we are not thinking in terms of antithesis, we might read this passage without realizing that it is structured as a conflict between two opposites. A similar technique appears in Proverbs 5:15–23, where five verses command faithful wedded love as an ideal and then four verses denigrate its opposite, namely, an adulterous lifestyle.

The principle of antithesis expands into structures even larger than individual passages. Proverbs 1–9 is a unified work of literature in which wisdom and folly (sometimes personified as women) are portrayed as rivals contending for the allegiance of a young man (representative of all people). The entire book of Ecclesiastes is organized as a grand structure of opposites—life under the sun (lived at a purely human and earthly level) and life above the sun (with God at the center).

The main lesson to carry away from the prevalence of antithesis is that we need to be vigilant in picking up on antithesis in individual proverbs and larger structures. Certainly we catch an overall sense that in a fallen world, good and evil, wisdom and folly, are engaged in a life-or-death struggle for the souls of people.

Comparison

A second principle found in the deep structure of biblical wisdom is comparison. Analogy (to be discussed in the following module) also compares two things to each other, but for the moment my subject is comparisons that use the formula or idea that one thing is *better* than another. Comparison of this type is known as a rhetorical form—a specific technique that became a standard convention in writing and also a persuasive strategy. Before I analyze that further, I place three examples before us:

- Wisdom "is more precious than jewels, / and nothing you desire can compare with her" (Prov. 3:15).
- "A good name is to be chosen rather than great riches, / and favor is better than silver or gold" (Prov. 22:1).
- "It is better to go the house of mourning / than to go to the house of feasting" (Eccl. 7:2).

All of these comparisons assert a hierarchy of values, as one thing is said to be better than another.

The observational format of such proverbs should not lull us into thinking that they are simple statements that do not require analysis. We need to ask such questions as the following: Exactly why is *A* declared to be better than *B?* What makes it better? What is the effect of the author's bringing in a comparison, when the value of the one could have been asserted by itself without the comparison? Why did the author choose that particular thing to compare the actual subject to (e.g., riches and jewels and a house of feasting in the verses quoted above)?

Analogy

A dictionary definition of analogy is "a comparison between two different things designed to show significant similarities." Analogy is based on an actual correspondence. The purpose of highlighting the correspondence is to use one area of human experience to shed light on another area of experience.

Like antithesis and comparison, analogy is part of the deep structure of biblical wisdom literature. It keeps coming up. Sometimes it appears in brief form: "Trusting in a treacherous man in time of trouble / is like a bad tooth or a foot that slips" (Prov. 25:19). At other times it appears in more expanded form: "As you do not know the way the spirit comes to the bones in the womb of a woman with child, so you do not know the work of God who makes everything" (Eccl. 11:5).

Sometimes we get a string of analogies, as in the following passage (Prov. 25:12–14):

> Like a gold ring or an ornament of gold
>   is a wise reprover to a listening ear.
> Like the cold snow in the time of harvest
>   is a faithful messenger to those who send him;
> Like clouds and wind without rain
>   is a man who boasts of a gift he does not give.

The analogies in poetic wisdom literature are mainly meta-phors and similes, and I have already covered these in the preceding chapter on poetry. I use the word "analogy" here to indicate the underlying principle and place it on a par with antithesis and comparison as a rhetorical form of wisdom literature. The word "analogy" is commonly used for wisdom literature, often instead of "metaphor" and "simile."

The task of interpretation is simple but very important. If *A* is declared to be like *B,* we need to analyze *how* they are alike. What truths emerge from the comparison between the two phenomena? How does the one area of life illuminate the other?

Incentive Formulas

Wisdom literature is filled with commands regarding what to do and what to avoid. But commands by themselves can seem dictatorial and tedious. Being master teachers, the writers of wisdom literature continuously give us an incentive to obey their commands. In this module I explore a specific wisdom literature formula in which a command or observation is linked with an incentive for heeding or obeying what has been commanded or observed. The following passage (Prov. 3:1–4) is an example of the wisdom formula of command-plus-reward:

> My son, do not forget my teaching,
>> but let your heart keep my commandments,
> for length of days and years of life
>> and peace they will add to you.
> Let not steadfast love and faithfulness forsake you;
>> bind them around your neck;
>> write them on the tablet of your heart.
> So you will find favor and good success
>> in the sight of God and man.

That is an example of an explicit incentive formula.

Usually the incentive takes a more subtle form. For example, the general tenor of the poetic proverbs in the Bible is to commend one course of action over another course of action. Upon reflection, we get the point that doing the right thing carries a reward, which in turn constitutes an incentive to choose wisely. The following passage (Prov. 9:10–12) is part of a speech uttered by a personified Wisdom:

> The fear of the LORD is the beginning of wisdom,
>> and the knowledge of the Holy One is insight.
> For by me your days will be multiplied,
>> and years will be added to your life.
> If you are wise, you are wise for yourself;
>> if you scoff, you alone will bear it.

The overall force is to give an incentive for choosing wisdom. In fact, the final appeal is based on enlightened self-interest.

The comparative proverbs in which something is said to be better than its alternative can also be fitted into the framework of incentive. The following verse (Eccl. 7:1) is an example: "A good name is better than precious ointment." We need to tease out the meaning of that statement, but the very fact that the author calls a good name "better" gives us an implied incentive to order our behavior according to the sage's observation.

At the most subtle level of all, the antithetical proverbs offer an implied incentive for choosing the right thing and disincentive for choosing the wrong thing. For example: "No ill befalls the righteous, / but the wicked are filled with trouble" (Prov. 12:21). In format, that is a simple observation, but if we ponder it aright, we are prompted to choose to be righteous because it carries a beneficial reward.

Proverb Formulas

Commentary on biblical proverbs and wisdom literature has multiplied the motifs and genres until the total reaches several dozen and collapses under its own weight. I therefore offer this module as something for readers to adopt if it seems helpful, but to pass over if it would induce overload.

The four ingredients listed below are found intermittently through the book of Proverbs. Sometimes all four form a tapestry in a single passage. At other times they are found two or three at a time.

- Summons to listen
- Admonitions
- Motivation for obeying
- Consequences of obedience

The following passage (Prov. 4:1–9) combines all four; I have identified the motifs in brackets immediately after the place where they appear:

Hear, O sons, a father's instruction,
   and be attentive [*summons to listen*], that you may
   gain insight,
for I give you good precepts; [*motivation*]
   do not forsake my teaching. [*admonition*]
When I was a son with my father,
   tender, the only one in the sight of my mother,
he taught me and said to me,
   "Let your heart hold fast my words;
   keep my commandments, and live.
   Get wisdom; get insight;
   do not forget, and do not turn away from the words
     of my mouth.

Do not forsake her [*admonition*], and she will keep you;
  [*consequences*]
    love her [*admonition*], and she will guard you.
      [*consequences*]
The beginning of wisdom is this: Get wisdom,
    and whatever you get, get insight.
Prize her highly [*admonition*], and she will exalt you;
    she will honor you [*consequences*] if you embrace her.
      [*admonition*]
She will place on your head a graceful garland;
    she will bestow on you a beautiful crown."
      [*consequences*]

The line between motivation and consequences is blurred in this passage, inasmuch as the consequences are an implied motivation to obey, but only if one is thinking in that vein.

In a slight variation of the foregoing elements, the pattern of combining a command with a reward appears. Here is an example (Prov. 3:3–4):

Let not steadfast love and faithfulness forsake you;
    bind them around your neck;
    write them on the tablet of your heart. [*command*]
So you will find favor and good success
    in the sight of God and man. [*reward*]

In yet another variation, sometimes we find not a command-plus-reward but an observation-plus-reward, as in the following example (Eccl. 4:9): "Two are better than one, because they have a good reward for their toil."

LEARNING BY DOING

This chapter has covered six forms or patterns in poetic wisdom literature: catalog, antithesis, comparison, analogy, incentive formulas, and a constellation of ingredients that appear together in various forms. The following two passages provide an opportunity to apply most of the categories that have been covered:

> My son, eat honey, for it is good,
>> and the drippings of the honeycomb are sweet to
>>> your taste.
> Know that wisdom is such to your soul;
>> if you find it, there will be a future,
>> and your hope will not be cut off.
> Lie not in wait as a wicked man against the dwelling of
> the righteous;
>> do no violence to his home;
>> for the righteous falls seven times and rises again,
>> but the wicked stumble in times of calamity.
>>> (Prov. 24:13–16)

> Sorrow is better than laughter,
>> for by sadness of face the heart is made glad.
> The heart of the wise is in the house of mourning,
>> but the heart of fools is in the house of mirth.
> It is better for a man to hear the rebuke of the wise
>> than to hear the song of fools.
> For as the crackling of thorns under a pot,
>> so is the laughter of the fools;
>> this also is vanity. (Eccl. 7:3–6)

Interpreting Proverbs

It is time to move from the description of what proverbs are to the question of how to interpret them. It is a difficult subject, partly because some proverbs state an observation that we know has many exceptions in real life. Here are three examples:

- "The plans of the diligent lead surely to abundance" (Prov. 21:5).
- "The reward for humility and fear of the LORD / is riches and honor and life" (Prov. 22:4).
- "Train up a child in the way he should go; / even when he is old he will not depart from it" (Prov. 22:6).

Two things need to be said immediately. First, only a small minority of proverbs fall into this category of seeming to promise more than we observe in real life. Second, even these proverbs express truth, so we should begin there and not immediately start to make qualifications. The prevailing practice in many circles is to begin with qualifications and thereby undermine confidence in the ability of proverbs to express truth.

In the discussion that follows, I lay out the principles of interpretation that I have found most useful when interpreting and teaching proverbs.

Real Life as the Best Context for Experiencing Proverbs

We encounter the proverbs of the Bible as individual entries in a collection of proverbs. In fact, when we read through an anthology like the book of Proverbs, we encounter one proverb after another. The distinctiveness of each one starts to get lost, and things start to become a blur. Of course, there is no other way to transact the business of conveying the proverbs of the wise men to us. But proverbs are not ultimately intended to express abstract truth that we grasp with our minds. They are intended to be a guide to godly and moral living. For that to happen, we need to take the proverbs out of the anthology and put them into the circumstances of life.

To shift gears for a moment, literature takes human experience as its subject. Literary authors (and the writers of biblical proverbs certainly are that) are gifted observers of life and human experience. They have the knack for observation. They are also the ones who are gifted to put their observations into words. Literature is the human race's testimony to its own experience, and proverbs do it as well as any other genre.

With this bit of literary theory in our awareness, we can turn to the proverbs of the Bible with new eyes. The proverbs are filled with authentic human experience. We are just not trained to look for it. What looks like a platitudinous idea is actually a snapshot of life. We encounter a wealth of human characters and actions in shorthand form as we read through the Bible's proverbs. To unpack that wealth, we need to allow the author's prompt to become a full-fledged picture. The unfailing confirmation that a proverb has spoken the truth is everyday life.

I note in passing that the Bible's wise men share a quality that John Bunyan displayed in his allegorical characters. Bunyan could bring a whole character into existence as both a social and a moral type with a mere name like Talkative or Pliable. In a similar way, the proverbs of the Bible put a character type or action before us with their succinct punch. The following are some examples:

- "The words of the whisperer are like delicious morsels; / they go down into the innermost parts of the body" (Prov. 18:8). The whisperer is the gossip and slanderer. The focus of the proverb, though, is not on the one who gossips but on the ones who hear. They love to hear gossip and share the secrets. We can confirm the parable in our own observations and experiences. A proverb is not a delivery system for an idea but a window onto the world.

- "'Bad, Bad,' says the buyer, / but when he goes away, then he boasts" (Prov. 20:14). Believe it or not, this proverb takes us on a shopping trip. The person described is someone with whom we would never choose to do business. He is a buyer who bullies his way to a good deal by denigrating the value of the merchandise to the seller. He is unscrupulous, deceptive, and domineering. Then he boasts about his bit of fraud to the folks back home.

- "Dead flies make the perfumer's ointment give off a stench; / so a little folly outweighs wisdom and honor" (Eccl. 10:1). This is the source of our familiar saying about "the fly in the ointment," referring to how a single fault or bad decision can destroy a person or enterprise. Literary tragedy presents the parallel of a good character brought to ruin by a single flaw of character or wrong choice. We see it regularly in life.

How does all this relate to interpretation of a proverb? Applying a proverb to a real-life situation is a form of interpretation. In the very act of applying the proverb, we show that we understand its meaning. We have illuminated the text, making its truth come alive.

What interpretive obligation does this impose on us? It requires us to be thinking of connections to real life. These connections might be our own experiences and observations, or they might involve keeping our antennae up for illustrations in the news or media. A good teaching strategy is to parcel out proverbs to class members a week ahead of the lesson or discussion and let them live with one or more proverbs for a week, looking for illustrations from life or the media. A lot of literary interpretation involves contextualizing a passage, so there is nothing unusual in what I am recommending. What is unusual is that I am suggesting real life as the context. When I teach literature, I tell my students that the most universal context for literature is not the author's life and times but human experience, including our own. The best confirmation of a proverb is a close look at what is going on around us.

One more exercise might prove helpful: go through a chapter in Proverbs (or ten verses of a chapter) and catalog the experiences and people that you meet when you look carefully for them. The range of events, situations, and people is greater than we usually think.

Ascertaining the Principle Embodied in a Proverb

Although a proverb is normally simple on the surface (as even its brevity suggests), interpreting proverbs can be more difficult than the initial simplicity might lead us to think. What I cover in this module is a prerequisite to further analysis that we need to do with a proverb. My subject is the need to identify the principle that underlies or permeates a proverb as a step that enables further interpretation.

The particular situation asserted in a proverb is usually a manifestation of something more universal. I can best explain that concept by giving four examples:

- "The lot is cast into the lap, / but its every decision is from the LORD" (Prov. 16:33). Casting lots is the external event; the principle asserted by the author's description of that event is God's sovereign providence in a person's life.
- "If one curses his father or his mother, / his lamp will be put out in utter darkness" (Prov. 20:20). Cursing one's parents is the situation or example; the principle is respect for parents and the judgment that God has built into the moral fabric of the universe against disrespect for parents and their authority (and by extension all authority).
- "A wise man's heart inclines him to the right, / but a fool's heart to the left" (Eccl. 10:2). The principle expressed by this observation is that people make their choice for good or evil as an expression of their inner being, or "heart." We choose right or wrong based on who we are spiritually. It is also implied that life is so constituted that people need to make a choice between good and evil as a condition of living.
- "If a tree falls to the south or to the north, / in the place where the tree falls, there it will lie" (Eccl. 11:3). The felling of a tree is the concrete situation; what that picture embodies is the principle of finality that accompanies many experiences in life. For many events, there is a no second chance. Of course, the ultimate finality is one's state of soul at the time of death.

A couple of qualifications or explanations need to be made. First, some proverbs carry their meaning on the surface, so the principle is virtually the same as the proverb. Even here, though, it is useful to state the principle. An example is Proverbs 14:34: "Righteousness exalts a nation, / but sin is a reproach to any people." The principle is that the honor or reproach of a nation depends on its righteousness or sin. The proverb states the principle.

Second, identifying the principle of a proverb is interpretive to a certain level, but it is not a complete interpretation. It *enables* fuller interpretation.

LEARNING BY DOING

The following proverbs give you an opportunity to identify underlying principles:

- "Whoever is slow to anger has great understanding, / but he who has a hasty temper exalts folly" (Prov. 14:29).
- "There is a way that seems right to a man, / but its end is the way to death" (Prov. 16:25).
- "The horse is made ready for the day of battle, / but the victory belongs to the LORD" (Prov. 21:31).
- "Better is a handful of quietness than two hands full of toil and a striving after wind" (Eccl. 4:6).

Ascertaining the Values, Virtues, and Vices in a Proverb

Because of the observational format of most proverbs, they often come across as ho-hum statements that lack urgency. Here is an example: "A worker's appetite works for him; / his mouth urges him on" (Prov. 16:26). An initial response might be that everyone knows that. So what?

Happily, there is a foolproof way to extract the profundity of a proverb. If we look closely at a proverb and analyze it with the following questions in mind, we will find that most proverbs implicitly express a viewpoint on the following three things:

- Values—What value(s) does this proverb commend or praise?
- Virtues—What virtue(s) does this proverb implicitly celebrate and command?
- Vices—What vice(s) does this proverb prohibit and denounce?

The following examples illustrate how this works.

- "Do not boast about tomorrow, / for you do not know what a day may bring" (Prov. 27:1). On the surface, this is a platitudinous statement that we never know what will happen during a day. The deeper profundity emerges when we apply my proposed questions. This proverb prohibits the vice of presumption; it commends humility before God's providence; and it exalts the value of relating to God in a way that acknowledges his sovereignty.
- "Let another praise you, and not your own mouth" (Prov. 27:2). Does this command about not bragging deal with an obnoxious social pest, or does its message run deeper than that? It runs deeper: this proverb prohibits self-praise and pride; it commends humility both within and in external conduct; and it implicitly asserts the value of humility as a condition of a good society.
- "One who is full loathes honey, / but to one who is hungry everything bitter is sweet" (Prov. 27:7). Here is an example of how important it is to begin by identifying the underlying principle. The proverb describes the two extremes of having too much and having too little. Both extremes destroy people's sense of judgment, leading

them to despise something good and accept or indulge in something deficient. The principle extends to more than food. The proverb implicitly praises the virtue and value of moderation between extremes, and encourages us to avoid extremes.

- "Like a bird that strays from its nest / is a man who strays from his home" (Prov. 27:8). The principle is the dangers of being cut loose from home values. The proverb commends the restraining influence of home and family, warns against the temptations that come when one is away from that restraining influence, and encourages the virtue of being vigilant when one journeys away from home.

I want to add a few tips for using the values-virtues-vices questions. First, the questions provide a menu of options. If a given proverb does not lend itself to one or two of the items, we should avoid forcing the situation. We should use the terms that apply to a given proverb. Second, sometimes a variation on my questions might seem more natural for a given proverb. For example, what does this proverb clarify? Alternatively, what course of action does this proverb want me to pursue?

LEARNING BY DOING

The following proverbs provide scope for applying the foregoing interpretive values-virtues-vices questions:

- "One gives freely, yet grows all the richer; / another withholds what he should give, and only suffers want" (Prov. 11:24).
- "The house of the wicked will be destroyed, / but the tent of the upright will flourish" (Prov. 14:11).

- "Faithful are the wounds of a friend; / profuse are the kisses of an enemy" (Prov. 27:6).
- "Sweet is the sleep of a laborer, whether he eats little or much, but the full stomach of the rich will not let him sleep" (Eccl. 5:12).
- "Be not quick in your spirit to become angry, / for anger lodges in the heart of fools" (Eccl. 7:9).

Interpreting Purely Descriptive Proverbs

The foregoing module has shown that even when proverbs state observations rather than commands, they have the force of a prescriptive statement. They implicitly commend and prohibit something, and thereby tell us how to conduct our lives. There are a few proverbs that do not have an obvious prescriptive orientation but instead *describe* situations that we are not intended to emulate. Here are four examples:

- "A bribe is like a magic stone in the eyes of the one who gives it; / wherever he turns he prospers" (Prov. 17:8).
- "The poor use entreaties, / but the rich answer roughly" (Prov. 18:23).
- "All a poor man's brothers hate him; / how much more do his friends go far from him" (Prov. 19:7).
- "Money answers everything" (Eccl. 10:19).

First, these observations about how things are in a fallen world are not offered as an encouragement to behave that way. These proverbs do not give rich people the right to push people around and assert their own interests without restraint. They do not condone bribery or shunning of the poor.

Second, if we place the situations described in these descriptive proverbs into the broader context of Scripture, we can see immediately that they portray character traits and conduct that we are expected to condemn. Once we have wielded that interpretive hand, even these proverbs that seem only to describe can yield a prescription for living. We are expected to repudiate bribery, abuse of power by the rich, and scorn for poor people.

Proverbs That Seem to Promise Too Much

There is, finally, a category of proverbs that make assertions that we do not find confirmed in our own experience in the way in which the proverb seems to assert. Almost all of these proverbs fall into the category of making unqualified claims for prosperity of the righteous and misfortune on the wicked. It is best to put four such proverbs on the table so we can see what we are talking about:

- "The upright will inhabit the land . . . / but the wicked will be cut off from the land" (Prov. 2:21–22).
- "No ill befalls the righteous, / but the wicked are filled with trouble" (Prov. 12:21).
- "Disaster pursues sinners, / but the righteous are rewarded with good" (Prov. 13:21).
- "When a man's ways please the LORD, / he makes even his enemies to be at peace with him" (Prov. 16:7).

First, we should not deny that these proverbs present a difficulty for interpretation. Second, this category is so small as to be, loosely speaking, statistically insignificant.

Nonetheless, we need to have a strategy for dealing with proverbs that seem to promise too much. The wrong path is to construct our whole attitude toward proverbs on the basis of this category. It is true that proverbs like these should not be viewed as absolutes or guaranteed promises, but they still obey the general rules of a proverb. All proverbs express general principles based on observation of life or on the nature of God's dealings with the human race. All proverbs express what is *typically* or *usually* true. The fact that there are exceptions does not mean that there is not a general rule. In fact, we have a proverb about "the exception that proves the rule." So the first requirement is that we not foreclose on the possibility that the difficult proverb states a truth.

We need to begin with the premise that we bring to every verse in the Bible, namely, that there is something here for me. My task is to find out what that something is. In real life, we do not discount a general rule simply because we know that there might be exceptions. We tell young people to study hard so they will succeed in school. The fact that sometimes success is not achieved does not invalidate the general correlation between studying and succeeding in school. It is true that often our enemies are not at peace with us, but the proverb quoted above nonetheless holds out a possibility that inspires us to try to make it happen.

Proverbs such as those quoted above tell us the truth about the character of God and how he desires us to live. We should embrace that truth. Additionally, while some of these proverbs speak of an outcome in this life, most of them leave undefined when and where the outcome will be realized. The outcome might be in the life to come. Or the promised reward might be spiritual rather than physical.

Yes, we need to avoid turning descriptions of a general principle into a guarantee or promise. But instead of dismissing optimistic proverbs, we should operate on the premise that good interpretive alternatives to such dismissal exist.

LEARNING BY DOING

The following passages fall into the category of proverbs discussed in this module and enable you to apply the principles that have been explained above:

"My son, do not forget my teaching,
    but let your heart keep my commandments,
for length of days and years of life
    and peace they will add to you" (Prov. 3:1–2).

"Everyone who is arrogant in heart is an abomination to
    the LORD;
    be assured, he will not go unpunished" (Prov. 16:5).

"The righteous falls seven times and rises again,
    but the wicked stumble in times of calamity" (Prov. 24:16).

From Simple Proverb to Prose Paragraph

Biblical wisdom literature comes to us in two main genres—poetry and prose. I had not realized until writing this guide that these two branches of wisdom literature are as distinctively different as they are. This difference is concealed because the generic label "wisdom literature" is applied to both, leading us naturally to think that they are the same. A main challenge that I faced while writing this chapter was to ascertain how prose wisdom literature is significantly similar to the basic proverb as discussed in the preceding four chapters.

In this chapter I tell the story of the stages by which, according to scholarly consensus, the simple proverb became the prose paragraph. This is a consideration of form rather than content, so it will not yield big dividends in regard to interpretation, but it is very important that we see the text before us with the greatest possible clarity.

How the Simple Proverb Started to Expand

In an earlier chapter I explored the basic form of the proverb, and I review that material briefly. The proverb is a simple unit consisting of one sentence: "Every word of God proves true" (Prov. 30:5).

When the one-sentence proverb appears in poetry, the verse form of parallelism almost inevitably produces a two-line proverb (even when the proverb remains a single sentence), as the following three verses (Prov. 15:16–18) demonstrate:

> Better is a little with the fear of the LORD
>> than great treasure and trouble with it.
> Better is a dinner of herbs where love is
>> than a fattened ox and hatred with it.
> A hot-tempered man stirs up strife,
>> but he who is slow to anger quiets contention.

I have quoted a string of verses to illustrate the additional point that the simplest format for proverbs is the catalog of self-contained proverbs. Presumably this is how the proverbs of the Bible began.

The simple proverb (including proverbs in a list) then moved in the direction of larger units. The first step toward such complexity involved making pairs of lines form the two halves of a parallel construction instead of just one line, as in the following passage (Prov. 24:19–20):

> Fret not yourself because of evildoers,
>> and be not envious of the wicked,
> for the evil man has no future;
>> the lamp of the wicked will be put out.

A further stage of complexity is the proverb cluster on a common theme. This can be relatively brief, as in the following example (Prov. 23:19–21), which I have printed in such a way as to show the stair-step arrangement of pairs of lines:

> Hear, my son, and be wise,
> and direct your heart in the way.
>> Be not among drunkards
>> or among gluttonous eaters of meat,
>>> for the drunkard and the glutton will come to poverty,
>>> and slumber will clothe them with rags.

Proverb clusters then expanded in the direction of larger and larger units. Here is a humorous portrait of the miserly host (Prov. 23:6–8):

> Do not eat the bread of a man who is stingy,
>> do not desire his delicacies,
> for he is like one who is inwardly calculating.
>> "Eat and drink!" he says to you,
>> but his heart is not with you.
> You will vomit up the morsels that you have eaten,
>> and waste your pleasant words.

There are many proverb clusters in the poetic book of Proverbs. Because the basic building block is still the simple proverb, it is easy to overlook a proverb cluster when we read it. To drive the point home, here is one more simple proverb cluster on the subject of seven things that are an abomination to God (Prov. 6:16–19):

> There are six things that the LORD hates,
>> seven that are an abomination to him:
> haughty eyes, a lying tongue,
>> and hands that shed innocent blood,
> a heart that devises wicked plans,
>> feet that make haste to run to evil,
> a false witness who breathes out lies,
>> and one who sows discord among brothers.

What is the takeaway value of knowing that the simple proverb underwent transmutations in the direction of greater complexity? To be good readers and teachers of the Bible, we need to see the text as it really is. The framework that I have presented is very helpful in seeing what a given passage consists of. In particular, we need to be aware that just because a passage consists of one-sentence and two-line proverbs does not mean that it is a catalog of self-contained proverbs; there could be larger units composed of individual proverbs.

LEARNING BY DOING

The following specimen passage (Prov. 22:22–29) will enable you to apply some of what has been presented in the foregoing module:

> Do not rob the poor, because he is poor,
>   or crush the afflicted at the gate,
> for the LORD will plead their cause
>   and rob of life those who rob them.
> Make no friendship with a man given to anger,
>   nor go with a wrathful man,
> lest you learn his ways
>   and entangle yourself in a snare.
> Be not one of those who give pledges,
>   who put up security for debts.
> If you have nothing with which to pay,
>   why should your bed be taken from under you?
> Do not move the ancient landmark
>   that your fathers have set.
> Do you see a man skillful in his work?
>   He will stand before kings;
>   he will not stand before obscure men.

Transition from Poetry to Prose

Prose is distinctly different from poetry. Its basic unit is the sentence, whereas that of poetry is the line. Poetry is succinct, whereas ordinary prose is expansive and sometimes diffuse. The syntax of poetry is short and even abrupt, and it usually does not make logical connections clear. Prose, however, pursues a continuous line of thought in which logical connections are indicated. Having described two alternatives, I need to serve notice that prose wisdom literature is a hybrid between the two tendencies just described.

I speak personally in saying that when I move from the poetic proverb covered thus far in this guide to the prose of Ecclesiastes, James, and the Sermon on the Mount, I initially wonder if the text can be considered wisdom literature in the sense that the book of Proverbs is wisdom literature. Certainly the prose books do not use the proverb as the basic building block to the degree that the book of Proverbs does.

When I opened my Bible to James, my eye quickly landed on the following passage as a good specimen to analyze:

> Come now, you who say, "Today or tomorrow we will go into such and such a town and spend a year there and trade and make a profit"—yet you do not know what tomorrow will bring. What is your life? For you are a mist that appears for a little time and then vanishes. Instead you ought to say, "If the Lord wills, we will live and do this or that." As it is, you boast in your arrogance. All such boasting is evil. So whoever knows the right thing to do and fails to do it, for him it is sin. (4:13–17)

For purposes of comparison, here is how poetic wisdom literature treats the same subject:

Do not boast about tomorrow,
> for you do not know what a day may bring. (Prov. 27:1)

We can begin by noting how the prose paragraph differs from the poetic version. The poetic proverb begins with a prescribed boundary in the form of a two-line unit. By contrast, the prose paragraph can be expanded as much as the author desires. The two-line version is succinct and stands out as being an extraordinary use of language, whereas the prose paragraph is somewhat less distinguishable from ordinary prose.

Can we consider the paragraph from James to be wisdom literature or proverbial literature? My answer is yes. The paragraph from James is not *quite* as far removed from conversation over a cup of coffee as the proverb is, but it is nonetheless obviously removed from such conversation. It is a special kind of prose that literary scholars call "prose poetry" or "poetic prose." It requires analysis to see the distinctive features of prose wisdom literature.

My own conclusion is that prose wisdom literature bears many resemblances to straight proverbs, in the following ways (and I will be analyzing the passage from James quoted above):

- Although the passage from James is composed around a central idea, it does not proceed as an essay does. The paragraph does not start with a thesis sentence but with a direct address to imaginary people. There is no thesis sentence with subpoints under it. If we look closely at the paragraph, we can see that it does have subpoints that *could* become separate paragraphs under a main thesis, but that is not how James thinks.

- The author handles the central idea by spinning out a series of individual thoughts related to it. The paragraph is not the *product* of thought the way expository prose is, but instead gives us the *process* of a person *thinking about* the main idea. The ordinary label for such writing is "meditation" or "reflection." It is like turning a prism in the light to see various angles.

- The paragraph makes more concentrated use of literary techniques than ordinary prose does. It begins with an apostrophe (addressing someone absent as though he were present). It incorporates imagined quotations from an imaginary person. There is a rhetorical question. There is a striking metaphor that compares a person's life to a vanishing mist.

- Although the prose paragraph is not as succinct as the two-line proverb, it is tighter in syntax (sentence structure) than ordinary conversation is. There are no transitions between the successive ideas. Approximately half of the paragraph consists of proverbs. Alternatively, we can say that the way James phrases matters is so aphoristic that much of the paragraph has entered our familiar storehouse of proverbs, even if the phrases fall just short of being proverbs.

- I end with a general impression: a paragraph of wisdom literature impresses us with a certain quality of compression. We are led to marvel that so much has been said in such little space.

LEARNING BY DOING

The following specimen paragraph (Matt. 5:43–49) will enable you to put the foregoing discussion into practice. Here are three prompts to aid your analysis:

- What makes the paragraph different from a paragraph in a typical essay written in expository prose?
- What traits of proverbial literature appear in the passage?
- In what ways does the passage fit the genre of meditative or reflective writing?

You have heard that it was said, "You shall love your neighbor and hate your enemy." But I say to you, Love your enemies and pray for those who persecute you, so that you may be sons of your Father who is in heaven. For he makes his sun rise on the evil and on the good, and sends rain on the just and on the unjust. For if you love those who love you, what reward do you have? Do not even the tax collectors do the same? And if you greet only your brothers, what more are you doing than others? Do not even the Gentiles do the same? You therefore must be perfect, as your heavenly Father is perfect.

The Structure of Prose Wisdom Literature beyond the Paragraph

I end by moving from individual paragraphs in wisdom literature to the broad structure of books or discourses in which they appear. In proverbial poetry, the organizing principle is (1) lists of individual proverbs and (2) clustering of proverbs in units that have a common subject. The basic principle is a cumulative one. Organization is disjointed rather than continuous.

Even though the paragraph in wisdom literature is a larger unit than the individual proverb or proverb cluster, it shares the basic format of discontinuity and an accumulation of self-contained units. Overwhelmingly, when we move from one paragraph to the next in prose wisdom literature, we leave the preceding subject behind and take up a new one. The underlying principle is a collection of individual paragraphs instead of individual proverbs. This differs from ordinary expository prose such as we find in an essay, where the paragraphs form a coherent whole and are related to each other as building blocks in a continuous line of thought.

The following two-paragraph sequence (James 1:12–18) captures the typical organization of prose wisdom literature:

> Blessed is the man who remains steadfast under trial, for when he has stood the test he will receive the crown of life, which God has promised to those who love him. Let no one say when he is tempted, "I am being tempted by God," for God cannot be tempted with evil, and he himself tempts no one. But each person is tempted when he is lured and enticed by his own desire. Then desire when it has conceived gives birth to sin, and sin when it is fully grown brings forth death.
>
> Do not be deceived, my beloved brothers. Every good gift and every perfect gift is from above, coming down from the Father of lights with whom there is no variation or shadow due to change. Of his own will he brought us forth by the word of truth, that we should be a kind of firstfruits of his creatures.

The first paragraph discusses temptation, and the second one asserts that every good gift comes from God. There is no connection between the two paragraphs, and no transition from the first to the second.

Summary

Proverbial literature in the Bible began as collections of individual proverbs. When these were anthologized, they became lists of proverbs. Then a movement toward more complex structures arose, first in proverbial poetry with its clusters of proverbs on a common theme. As the impulse toward expansiveness set in, the prose paragraph became the most natural vehicle. But within the individual prose paragraph and the larger prose wisdom books (Ecclesiastes and James) or discourses (such as the Sermon on the Mount), much of the original paradigm remained, producing discourses that are midway between poetic proverbs and ordinary prose.

Larger Units

This chapter focuses on what the paragraphs in prose wisdom literature are like. These units fall into a taxonomy of types, and it is helpful to know what these are. When we name these types, it is obvious that some of them exist in the book of Proverbs and the poetic parts of Ecclesiastes as well as prose wisdom literature. This chapter clarifies that too.

Narrative

The essential feature of narrative is that it recounts action. Wisdom literature sometimes falls into a narrative format. The book of Ecclesiastes provides examples. The following passage (2:4–6) is an excerpt from a longer unit in which the author tells the story of his quest to find satisfaction in pleasure and acquisition of material things:

> I made great works. I built houses and planted vineyards for myself. I made myself gardens and parks, and planted in them all kinds of fruit trees. I made myself pools from which to water the forest of growing trees.

This passage tells us what the author did, so it is a narrative.

Narrative can be more subtle than a straightforward recounting of action, and in these cases it is possible to overlook the narrative element. Here is an example from James (1:23–24):

> For if anyone is a hearer of the word and not a doer, he is like a man who looks intently at his natural face in a mirror. For he looks at himself and goes away and at once forgets what he was like.

Technically this is a simile, but as the simile keeps expanding, we experience it as a brief narrative of someone looking in a mirror and then walking away in a gesture of thoughtlessness. We can speak of *a narrative aspect* to such a passage.

We might think that a collection of proverbs features only lists of proverbs or proverb clusters, but this is untrue. The book of Proverbs uses the format of individual proverbs, but there are nonetheless embedded narratives. Proverbs 7:6–23 comes alive in our imagination as a full-fledged temptation story. Proverbs 8:22–31 is a mini-creation story. Proverbs 24:30–32 likewise tells a story in brief compass:

> I passed by the field of a sluggard,
>> by the vineyard of a man lacking sense,
> and behold, it was all overgrown with thorns;
>> the ground was covered with nettles,
>> and its stone wall was broken down.
> Then I saw and considered it;
>> I looked and received instruction.

The passage re-creates the action of a walk in the neighborhood, with emphasis on seeing an overgrown field and then being prompted to reflect on the bad effects of sloth. The passage has the sequence of a story in which one thing leads to the next.

I do not want to overstate the case, but it is important to be aware of how often as we are reading wisdom literature we relive brief stories. Once we are alerted to this narrative flavor, we will see that even individual proverbs can become narrative moments in our imagination. An example is Proverbs 11:26: "The people curse him who holds back grain, / but a blessing is on the head of him who sells it." If we allow that verse to take root in our imagination, we first picture a hoarder holding back grain in the hope that prices will rise and he can make a killing. A brief story unfolds in our minds of desperate people milling around outside the closed door of a grocery store. Then we picture the action of a generous person selling grain to needy and grateful buyers, and the latter walking away with a bag of grain and with goodwill toward the seller.

Proverbial literature is characterized by compression. Individual proverbs are intended to be a prompt to our imagination, as we relate a proverb to real life as we know it. It is no wonder that we experience many brief narratives as we read wisdom literature. The essence of narrative is an action or plot, but we cannot have that without characters and settings. We encounter many characters and inferred settings as we read wisdom literature.

LEARNING BY DOING

We will see the narrative element in wisdom literature only if we take time to ponder the material and look for a story line. The following words of Jesus (Matt. 7:24–27), will enable you to analyze the narrative element in wisdom literature:

> Everyone then who hears these words of mine and does
> them will be like a wise man who built his house on the

rock. And the rain fell, and the floods came, and the winds blew and beat on that house, but it did not fall, because it had been founded on the rock. And everyone who hears these words of mine and does not do them will be like a foolish man who built his house on the sand.

Vignette

The vignette is a close relative of the brief narrative discussed in the preceding module. Sometimes it is a tossup as to whether a unit is a brief narrative or a vignette. Dictionary definitions of vignette are all over the board, but there is a consensus that a literary vignette (as distinct from a vignette in theater and painting) can be defined in the following terms:

- a descriptive sketch
- a short scene or incident
- a description that focuses on one moment or captures the essence of a character, setting, or object

The book of Proverbs contains striking vignettes that stay in our memory the way an individual proverb does. The following passage (Prov. 6:6–8) is a vignette of the industrious ant:

Go to the ant, O sluggard;
 consider her ways, and be wise.
Without having any chief,
 officer, or ruler,
she prepares her bread in summer
and gathers her food in harvest.

Ecclesiastes 2:22–23 is a vignette of the workaholic:

What has a man from all the toil and striving of heart with which he toils beneath the sun? For all his days are full of sorrow, and his work is a vexation. Even in the night his heart does not rest. This also is vanity.

In Matthew 6:2, Jesus provides a vignette of people who give ostentatiously to religious causes in such a way as to draw attention to themselves:

Thus, when you give to the needy, sound no trumpet before you, as the hypocrites do in the synagogues and in the streets, that they may be praised by others. Truly, I say to you, they have received their reward.

A vignette requires no special rules of interpretation. We simply need to identify a vignette so we can concentrate on it as a separate unit. A vignette shines the spotlight on a specific subject and captures it in its essence, and that is the same principle that governs the proverb as a literary form.

LEARNING BY DOING

The first obligation that a vignette places on us is to determine the boundaries of the unit, thereby isolating the passage for consideration by itself; that task has been performed by the printing of the following passage as a vignette.

The second activity is to ponder the exact subject that has been sketched, in an awareness that a proverb portrays the essence of a subject. Then we need to reach a conclusion as to what edification we are intended to carry away from our encounter with the sketch. The following passage (Prov. 26:13–16) is a case in point:

> The sluggard says, "There is a lion in the road!
>   There is a lion in the streets!"
> As a door turns on its hinges,
>   so does a sluggard on his bed.
> The sluggard buries his hand in the dish;
>   it wears him out to bring it back to his mouth.
> The sluggard is wiser in his own eyes
>   than seven men who can answer sensibly.

Meditation or Reflection

Meditation is a standard literary form, not limited to wisdom literature. As a literary form, a meditation is defined as a piece of writing that expresses a writer's thoughts on a subject. Often the effect is that of entering into the mind of someone who is "thinking things through."

A written meditation is not so much the end *product* of thought as it is the *process of thinking*. Of course, the author of a piece of writing does not write only for himself but for a reader, so we need to add to our definition that a literary meditation is offered as a guide to others in contemplating a given subject. As we read a reflective piece, we share the author's thinking and insights.

The literary genre of meditation or reflection enters wisdom literature primarily in two ways. Individual proverbs require pondering or reflection. Sometimes this analysis is required simply to figure out the meaning of the proverb, and we would do well to remember that the author of Proverbs offers the riddle as a synonym for proverb. A proverb is a meditative form. We cannot read wisdom literature as we read a story or even a poem. Our focus needs to be more concentrated on individual statements that need to be applied to life after we have unpacked what they mean. I found useful a scholar's claim that a good proverb is not intended to put an end to thought but to be a beginning to further thought.

The second relevance of the meditative genre is that it is one of the forms that make up prose wisdom literature. The aim of this chapter is to provide a taxonomy of types of units that we find when reading books like Ecclesiastes and James.

The book of Ecclesiastes contains numerous units that are reflections on a subject. I myself find it easy to picture the author as sitting down at the end of a day and writing a journal-type meditation on something that he encountered during the day. The following passage (Eccl. 4:9–12) is a meditation on the advantages that come from companionship and marriage:

> Two are better than one, because they have a good reward for their toil. For if they fall, one will lift up his fellow. But woe to him who is alone when he falls and has not another to lift him up! Again, if two lie together, they keep warm, but how can one keep warm alone? And though a man might prevail against one who is alone, two will withstand him—a threefold cord is not quickly broken.

We can break down the rules of interpretation for a reflective piece as follows:

- Our first task is to identify the subject of the meditation. The quoted paragraph from Ecclesiastes 4 is about the advantages of having a companion or spouse as compared to being solitary and on one's own.
- Having identified the subject, we need to follow the author's train of thought, perhaps numbering the successive thoughts that are put before us. The sequence in the quoted passage is as follows: (1) the thesis or main idea asserted; (2) proof in the form of picturing what

happens when one falls in the company of a companion as contrasted to being solitary; (3) a second illustration of the superiority of companionship over solitude in regard to being warm or cold; (4) a third proof in the form of having protection from an attacker as opposed to being easily vanquished when alone; (5) a concluding aphorism or saying that clinches the main point.

Overall we can compare tracing the sequence of thought in a meditative piece to turning a prism in the light.

There is a counterpart to a meditation couched in a prose paragraph, namely, a list of proverbs embodied in poetic form. Only with proverb clusters does a book like Proverbs give us a meditation on a single subject, but when we read a sequence of self-contained proverbs, we conduct the exercise that resembles what we do with a prose meditation. We assume that the collector of the proverbs is sharing a sequence of ideas or observations, just as the author of Ecclesiastes does with a paragraph unified by a single topic. We are intended to carefully consider each proverb, in effect meditating on it.

LEARNING BY DOING

The following meditation on the subject of temptation (James 1:12–15) will provide a test case for how to deal with a piece of meditative wisdom literature:

> Blessed is the man who remains steadfast under trial, for
> when he has stood the test he will receive the crown of
> life, which God has promised to those who love him. Let
> no one say when he is tempted, "I am being tempted by

God," for God cannot be tempted with evil, and he himself tempts no one. But each person is tempted when he is lured and enticed by his own desire. Then desire when it has conceived gives birth to sin, and sin when it is fully grown brings forth death.

Observation or Description

In an earlier chapter that discussed the proverb at its core, I noted that the two basic forms used in the individual proverb are the observation and the command. Those two formats also appear in a taxonomy of the categories of paragraphs in prose wisdom literature. In some paragraphs, the wise man shares observations of things he has seen. Alternatively, we can say that the author *describes* a situation.

In the following passage (Eccl. 5:13–17), the author shares what he has observed about the futility and self-destructiveness that people bring on themselves when they are obsessed with making money:

There is a grievous evil that I have seen under the sun: riches were kept by their owner to his hurt, and those riches were lost in a bad venture. And he is father of a son, but he has nothing in his hand. As he came from his mother's womb he shall go again, naked as he came, and shall take nothing for his toil that he may carry away in his hand. This also is a grievous evil: just as he came, so shall he go, and what gain is there to him who toils for the wind? Moreover, all his days he eats in darkness in much vexation and sickness and anger.

The passage is meditative in nature, as covered in the preceding module, but the additional point here is that the format is descriptive and observational, being an account of what the author has "seen."

No special interpretive rules accompany the descriptive format. Nonetheless, an important aspect of Bible interpretation is to see accurately the exact nature of the text that is before us. Description is different from narration (previously covered) and command (about to be discussed).

Command or Exhortation

Just as individual proverbs often take the form of a command, prose paragraphs can also follow that format. Because writers of wisdom literature shuttle back and forth among various formats, and because the continuous presence of proverbs functions as a kind of background chorus, it is quite possible not to shift gears as we move from one format to another. The final entry in my taxonomy of types of paragraphs in prose wisdom literature is the command. The following passage (James 5:7–9) strikes us as entirely familiar in wisdom literature:

> Be patient, therefore, brothers, until the coming of the Lord. See how the farmer waits for the precious fruit of the earth, being patient about it, until it receives the early and the late rains. You also, be patient. Establish your hearts, for the coming of the Lord is at hand. Do not grumble against one another, brothers, so that you may not be judged; behold, the Judge is standing at the door.

Here is another example of the command format (Eccl. 5:1–3):

> Guard your steps when you go to the house of God. To draw near to listen is better than to offer the sacrifice of

fools, for they do not know that they are doing evil. Be not rash with your mouth, nor let your heart be hasty to utter a word before God, for God is in heaven and you are on earth. Therefore let your words be few. For a dream comes with much business, and a fool's voice with many words.

Summary

This chapter has dealt with matters that do not primarily touch on interpretation but with the format in which the content is packaged. That does not mean this chapter is unimportant. In the nineteenth century, literary figure Matthew Arnold claimed that the aim of every discipline, including literature, is "to see the object as in itself it really is." It is important to see the precise nature of the units that we encounter in wisdom literature.

A Miscellany of Wisdom
Literature Forms

One thing that this volume shares with other books in this series of guided studies to the genres of the Bible is that when we start to look closely at the literary forms and techniques of a chosen genre, the list of specific literary forms within that genre keeps expanding. Despite the large number of forms already covered, further ones remain to be explored. I have labeled this material a "miscellany," a literary term that refers to a varied collection of individual literary genres or works.

This miscellany can be related to the preceding chapter in the following way: the larger units covered in chapter 6 are a staple in the prose wisdom books and are common (though not a staple) in the poetic wisdom books. The forms covered in the current chapter are important but appear less frequently than such forms as narrative, description, and meditation covered in the preceding chapter. We might think of these further forms as being a more specialized category than the others in the sense that we encounter them less often.

Beatitude

The beatitude was an important literary form in ancient cultures. Homer's *Odyssey*, for example, contains many domestic beatitudes. A beatitude is a pronouncement of blessing, phrased in the formula "blessed is" or "blessed are." To some degree, the formal pronouncement of a blessing confers the very quality that is pronounced. There are two basic formats for a beatitude. The first is a simple pronouncement of blessing: "Blessed is he who is generous to the poor" (Prov. 14:21). The second adds the promise of a reward: "Blessed are the peacemakers, for they shall be called sons of God" (Matt. 5:9).

The book of Proverbs contains a dozen beatitudes. Here are three of them:

- "Blessed is the one who finds wisdom, / and the one who gets understanding" (3:13).
- "Blessed is the one who listens to me" (8:34).
- "Blessed is he who trusts in the LORD" (16:20).

Even when a proverb does not pronounce blessedness, as we read the Old Testament proverbs we continuously realize that the conduct and character traits that we are commanded to obey lead to blessedness, so we can say that the *spirit* of the beatitude permeates wisdom literature.

The opening section of Jesus' Sermon on the Mount gives us the famous passage known to posterity as "the beatitudes." The first one states, "Blessed are the poor in spirit, for theirs is the kingdom of heaven" (Matt. 5:3). The beatitudes of Jesus are by no means limited to the Sermon on the Mount but are sprinkled throughout the Gospels, where they are often referred to as the sayings of Jesus.

What are the interpretive implications that attach to the beatitude? Before we analyze a beatitude, we need to receive it and let its impact settle into our mind and heart. It is momentous to receive the blessing of God, and the evocative form of the beatitude highlights that. We need first to receive the blessing and let it bathe us. Additionally, a beatitude carries with it an implied command to emulate the type of character on whom the blessing is pronounced, so we can receive a beatitude with a resolve to be in the group that is named as being eligible for the blessing that is pronounced.

In addition to these elements of reception and resolve, we need to note the precise nature of the beatitude. It might be a simple pronouncement of blessing, or it might combine that with a promised reward. Then we need to ponder the exact nature of the person who is said to be blessed, and the exact nature of the reward (if one is stated).

Finally, we need to be aware of a slight difference between the Old Testament beatitude and the New Testament one. The beatitudes in the Old Testament wisdom literature are statements of blessing only, unaccompanied by a reward. The general tenor of these proverbs is that they pronounce blessing on those in the believing community who live under God's covenant rule. The nature of the blessing is left unstated.

By contrast, many New Testament beatitudes are accompanied by a promised reward, and the important thing about that reward is that usually it is eschatological in nature, to be fulfilled in the age to come. James 1:12 illustrates this type (as do Jesus' beatitudes in the Sermon on the Mount): "Blessed is the man who remains steadfast under trial, for when he has stood the test he will receive the crown of life, which God has promised to those who love him."

LEARNING BY DOING

The following four proverbs will enable you to apply what has just been presented. The second two are not phrased as beatitudes, but they operate in a way similar to that of beatitudes. You can profitably analyze what aspects of a beatitude can be applied to the proverbs that commend a certain person or behavior without pronouncing a blessing.

- "Blessed is he who keeps the law" (Prov. 29:18).
- "Blessed are the pure in heart, for they shall see God" (Matt. 5:8).
- "He who finds a wife finds a good thing / and obtains favor from the LORD" (Prov. 18:22).
- "A harvest of righteousness is sown in peace by those who make peace" (James 3:18).

Humor

Is wisdom literature funny? No, but it is has its moments of lightness and laughter, and it is important that we not suppress humor when it is present. Most of the humorous proverbs describe character types and situations that go by the name of situation comedy. The following are examples of humorous proverbs:

- "Like a gold ring in a pig's snout / is a beautiful woman without discretion" (Prov. 11:22). The humor arises when we picture the pig's snout with a gold ring in it.
- "Like a madman who throws firebrands, arrows, and death / is the man who deceives his neighbor and says, 'I am only joking!'" (Prov. 26:18–19).

- "Whoever blesses his neighbor with a loud voice, / rising early in the morning, / will be counted as cursing" (Prov. 27:14). It is unclear whether the proverb is about the trials of *having* a cheerful early-rising roommate or neighbor, or *being* a cheerful early riser and having one's cheerfulness spurned.
- "If the serpent bites before it is charmed, / there is no advantage to the charmer" (Eccl. 10:11). We are to picture someone who pretends to put on a "good show" but overlooks the obvious; the event pictured belongs to the category that makes it onto television shows that feature funny home videos.

What conclusions might we draw from the occasional presence of humor in wisdom literature? The wise men who wrote wisdom literature had a keen eye for human personality and everyday life. They can be trusted to see what is expressed by the French formula *la comédie humaine*—the human comedy, or human nature with its quirks and folly.

LEARNING BY DOING

A joke requires figuring out, and the following proverbs may require unpacking before you see the humor in the situation. It is important that you give these examples a try; if necessary, consult a commentary or conduct a computer search. Sometimes the humor emerges if we simply picture what the author puts before us.

- "The sluggard says, 'There is a lion outside! / I shall be killed in the streets!'" (Prov. 22:13).
- "Like an archer who wounds everybody / is one who hires a passing fool or drunkard" (Prov. 26:10).

- "Whoever meddles in a quarrel not his own / is like one who takes a passing dog by the ears" (Prov. 26:17).
- "A continual dripping on a rainy day / and a quarrelsome wife are alike" (Prov. 27:15).

Encomium

The encomium is one of the great genres in the Bible, and it can be trusted to give us an uplift every time we read an example. An encomium is a poem or prose piece written *in praise of* a character type or an abstract quality. Psalm 1 praises a general character type, namely, the godly person. First Corinthians 13 praises the abstract quality love.

An encomium conducts its praise according to a prescribed format. That format is as follows (and a given encomium might omit one or two of the motifs):

- an introduction to the subject that will be praised (sometimes accompanied by a definition of the subject or a preliminary commendation of the subject)
- the distinguished and ancient ancestry of the subject
- a catalog or description of the praiseworthy acts and qualities of the subject
- the indispensable or superior nature of the subject (sometimes accomplished by contrasting the subject to its opposite or stating the rewards that accompany the quality or way of life of the subject)
- a conclusion that urges the reader to emulate the subject

Variations of these motifs are possible, but even when we find exceptions, we will be in a position to see what is happening more accurately if we know the general pattern. For example, if the subject is presented so winsomely that we would naturally want to emulate it, a formal command to imitate the model might be superfluous.

The greatest example of an encomium in biblical wisdom literature is the poem in praise of the virtuous wife in Proverbs 31:10–31. A sidelight on this poem is that it is an acrostic poem in which the successive verses begin with the letters of the Hebrew alphabet in consecutive order. The poem begins with a formal introduction that announces the subject and praises her worth: "An excellent wife who can find? / She is far more precious than jewels" (v. 10). As always in an encomium, the subject is not a specific person but a generalized character type. The poet dispenses with the motif of distinguished ancestry and concentrates solely on the praiseworthy virtues and actions of the ideal wife. The poem concludes with a prayer or wish that the virtuous wife might be rewarded: "Give her of the fruit of her hands, / and let her works praise her in the gates" (v. 31).

The other encomia in biblical wisdom literature occur in the book of Proverbs. They praise the quality of wisdom and are found in Proverbs 3:13–20 and Proverbs 8. In the latter example, a personified Wisdom commends herself in the standard encomiastic formulas of listing her praiseworthy acts and rewards for those who follow wisdom. There is even a variation on the motif of distinguished ancestry (vv. 22–31). Intermittently in this poem, the superiority of wisdom over folly is asserted.

Character Sketch or Portrait

The character sketch has been around since time immemorial. It still occasionally makes an appearance as an assignment in high school and college writing courses. The ancients loved this genre and called it simply *the character*. English author Geoffrey Chaucer immortalized the form in his prologue to *The Canterbury Tales*, where he assembled the cast of characters for his masterpiece.

It is in the nature of this genre to paint portraits of general character types rather than specific individuals. Of course, the author might be aided in the composition by a real-life model. The goal of a character sketch is the same as that of a proverb—to capture the essence of an experience in a very brief compass. A character sketch is not designed to impart new information but to codify and bring to awareness what we already know and have observed.

In keeping with a paradigm noted earlier in this guide, the portraits that we glean from wisdom literature range from a single proverb to full-fledged portraits that would be right at home in a literary compilation of character portraits. The following passage (Prov. 26:13–16) paints a portrait of the sluggard, or lazy person, by picturing typical actions of such a person—finding excuses not to get up in the morning, turning over in bed instead of getting up, not finishing tasks, and commending himself for his sluggish lifestyle:

> The sluggard says, "There is a lion in the road!
>   There is a lion in the streets!"
> As a door turns on its hinges,
>   so does a sluggard on his bed.
> The sluggard buries his hand in the dish;
>   it wears him out to bring it back to his mouth.
> The sluggard is wiser in his own eyes
>   than seven men who can answer sensibly.

A character sketch achieves its purpose if the portrait strikes us as true to life. The type comes alive through a few deft details, and the truthfulness is confirmed in our own experience and observation.

Some of the character sketches are more ambitious than the one just considered. Proverbs 23:29–35 captures the typical actions of a drunkard. The portrait of the virtuous wife (Prov. 31:10–31) can be considered a character sketch as well as an encomium. The great "set piece" in this genre is the portrait of the aging person in Ecclesiastes 12:1–8, where we are led to picture the physical effects of aging on the body. It is a highly metaphoric picture in which (for example) a stooped upper torso is pictured as "strong men [that are] bent" and the loss of teeth as "grinders [that] cease because they are few" (v. 3). Even more famous is the portrait of the ideal follower of Jesus that emerges from the beatitudes of Matthew 5:2–12.

Wisdom literature contains portraits that might not quite rank as a character sketch but that will come alive to us if we place them into that category. I offer the following portrait of the praying man as an example (James 5:16b–18):

> The prayer of a righteous person has great power as it is working. Elijah was a man with a nature like ours, and he prayed fervently that it might not rain, and for three years and six months it did not rain on the earth. Then he prayed again, and heaven gave rain, and the earth bore its fruit.

The book of Proverbs offers a variation on the pattern of the character sketch as I have delineated it. We encounter numerous character types diffused throughout the book of Proverbs in individual freestanding proverbs. Examples include the foolish person, the wise person, the sluggard, the greedy person, the hothead, and the drunkard. To compile a sketch from these individual fragments is easy: all we need to do is work our way through the book of Proverbs and compile our own proverb cluster. I have found that this can actually be done rather quickly. The following proverb cluster yields a composite sketch of the diligent worker:

- "Whoever works his land will have plenty of bread" (12:11).
- "The hand of the diligent will rule" (12:24).
- "In all toil there is profit" (14:23).

- "The plans of the diligent lead surely to abundance" (21:5).
- "Whoever tends a fig tree will eats its fruit, / and he who guards his master will be honored" (27:18).

These individual details yield a picture of a general character type conceived in terms of what the industrious worker does and the results that follow from diligence. It is in the nature of literature to put examples before us—positive examples to emulate and negative ones to avoid. Often the proverbs of the Bible put both together in the form of an antithetic parallelism: "He who gathers in summer is a prudent son, / but he who sleeps in harvest is a son who brings shame" (Prov. 10:5).

LEARNING BY DOING

A character sketch is designed to put a universal character type before us in such a way that we say to ourselves, "Yes, this is true to life." The author sketches out the portrait with typical traits, actions, and outcomes. The following portrait of the wise son (Prov. 4:20–27) will enable you to analyze these features:

> My son, be attentive to my words;
>   incline your ear to my sayings.
> Let them not escape from your sight;
>   keep them within your heart.
> For they are life to those who find them,
>   and healing to all their flesh.
> Keep your heart with all vigilance,
>   for from it flow the springs of life.
> Put away from you crooked speech,
>   and put devious talk far from you.

> Let your eyes look directly forward,
>   and your gaze be straight before you.
> Ponder the path of your feet;
>   then all your ways will be sure.
> Do not swerve to the right or to the left;
>   turn your foot away from evil.

Having assembled the portrait, we need to ponder what lessons we are expected to carry away from having looked at the character.

Satire and Rebuke

The wisdom literature of the Bible has a continuous satiric thread, and we cannot fully succeed with this body of literature without a grasp of this important genre. Satire is an attack on human vice or folly. Experts on wisdom literature also use the category of "rebuke," and that is a good synonym for "satire." A full-fledged satire has four ingredients:

- an object of attack or rebuke
- a satiric vehicle in which the exposure of vice or folly is embodied
- an explicit or implied satiric norm (the standard of correctness by which the criticism is being conducted)
- a satiric tone, which is either biting or light

The satire that we find in wisdom literature exists on a continuum ranging from full-fledged satiric passages on one end to single proverbs on the other. The following portrait of people who are ostentatious in their religious life (with emphasis on financial giving) falls in the middle of the continuum (Matt. 6:1–4):

[1] Beware of practicing your righteousness before other people in order to be seen by them, for then you will have no reward from your Father who is in heaven.

[2] Thus, when you give to the needy, sound no trumpet before you, as the hypocrites do in the synagogues and in the streets, that they may be praised by others. Truly, I say to you, they have received their reward. [3] But when you give to the needy, do not let your left hand know what your right hand is doing, [4] so that your giving may be in secret. And your Father who sees in secret will reward you.

The four ingredients of satire are clear:

- Object of attack or rebuke: people who perform religious acts (in this case giving to the poor) in such a way as to call attention to themselves and be praised for their generosity.
- Satiric vehicle: an opening proverb (v. 1) followed by a humorous and exaggerated portrait (v. 2).
- Satiric norm: performing deeds of generosity in secret; this is the principle that the ostentatious givers violate.
- Tone: because of the humorous portrait of hiring a band to play as the hypocrites do, the tone is light, as the ostentatious people become an example of laughable folly.

James' famous denunciation of prejudice against the poor (2:1–7) is an example of a more expanded satiric passage:

[1] My brothers, show no partiality as you hold the faith in our Lord Jesus Christ, the Lord of glory. [2] For if a man wearing a gold ring and fine clothing comes into your assembly, and a poor man in shabby clothing also comes in, [3] and if you pay attention to the one who wears the

fine clothing and say, "You sit here in a good place," while you say to the poor man, "You stand over there," or, "Sit down at my feet," [4] have you not then made distinctions among yourselves and become judges with evil thoughts? [5] Listen, my beloved brothers, has not God chosen those who are poor in the world to be rich in faith and heirs of the kingdom, which he has promised to those who love him? [6] But you have dishonored the poor man. Are not the rich the ones who oppress you, and the ones who drag you into court? [7] Are they not the ones who blaspheme the honorable name by which you were called?

Here is how the passage unfolds its form and content according to the four ingredients of satire:

- Object of attack: showing partiality against poor people in deference to rich people.
- Satiric vehicle: a picture of the partiality that the author is condemning, accompanied by direct denunciation and pointed rhetorical questions.
- Satiric norm: not showing partiality, as stated in the opening proverb (v. 1).
- Satiric tone: serious and condemnatory.

The foregoing two examples show that there are full-fledged satiric passages in the wisdom literature of the Bible. The main application, though, is the continuous satiric undertow that we find in the Bible's individual proverbs. Here is a proverb that I will analyze to illustrate what I mean: "It is better to be of a lowly spirit with the poor / than to divide the spoil with the proud" (Prov. 16:19). The object of rebuke is pride. The satiric vehicle is an antithetic proverb. The norm or standard of correctness is being humble. The tone is objective, inasmuch as the author does not overtly condemn pride, but certainly the proverb leaves no room for levity.

In chapter 4, I noted that individual proverbs usually explicitly or implicitly *command* something and *forbid* something. Satire is getting at this same situation. The forbidden act or character trait is satirically exposed. The command is the satiric norm.

I do not claim that we need to try to find satire in individual proverbs all the time. It is a useful analytic tool if we want to get maximum mileage out of a proverb. Most important is that we be aware of how continuously the wisdom literature of the Bible is criticizing what is wrong and setting a positive norm or antidote against it.

LEARNING BY DOING

The following passage (Prov. 24:30–34) will enable you to identify the four elements of satire. In regard to the satiric norm, although usually it appears explicitly somewhere in the passage, this is not automatic; sometimes we need to infer the standard by which the object of attack is rebuked.

I passed by the field of a sluggard,
 by the vineyard of a man lacking sense,
and behold, it was all overgrown with thorns;
 the ground was covered with nettles,
 and its stone wall was broken down.
Then I saw and considered it;
 I looked and received instruction.
A little sleep, a little slumber,
 a little folding of the hands to rest,
and poverty will come upon you like a robber,
 and want like an armed man.

The Rhetoric of Persuasion

It might initially seem a stretch to devote a whole chapter to persuasion in wisdom literature. After all, wisdom literature was a form of instruction and teaching in the ancient world. Nonetheless, wisdom literature does not resemble classroom teaching as we know it. There is much that is distinctive about it as a form of teaching, and one of these distinctives is its persuasive cast.

The technical term that scholars use for the material that I cover in this chapter is "rhetoric." Rhetoric means two things in literary criticism and communication—a set of techniques and the strategy by which a writer achieves a persuasive aim. In this case, the two are the same enterprise. I will explore how the wisdom writers pursue their persuasive goal by means of specific techniques. The subject of this chapter is the rhetoric of persuasion in the wisdom literature of the Bible.

Verbal Beauty

I begin with a subject that perhaps only a literary scholar would put on the agenda. Proverbs are an example of verbal beauty. So are the haunting and riveting paragraphs in prose wisdom literature. Writers of proverbs and prose wisdom have a way with words that most people lack. Virtually all of this guide up to this point has been an exploration of what elevates wisdom literature above everyday discourse and makes it stand out in our minds. I simply assume that the point is established.

How can verbal beauty be a technique of persuasion? Beauty of expression adds to the impact of an utterance. Something that is well phrased simply makes a greater impact than material that is prosaic. A really good proverb or prose paragraph not only expresses an insight but actually *produces* it—"a flash of insight," as one scholar calls it.

In addition to the captivating quality of a proverb as we read or hear it, there is the aspect of being remembered. The staying power of a proverb in our minds prolongs its "shelf life" and keeps yielding a harvest of persuasion over the long haul. The more often we remember a proverb, the more persuasive it is in our life.

The classic formula for the verbal beauty of proverbial literature comes from the book of Ecclesiastes. In 12:10, the author tells us that he "sought to find words of delight." This hints at an additional aspect of the topic of the persuasiveness of wisdom literature. If something is delightful, we find it winsome. We want to embrace it. If the object in question is a work of literature, we find it entertaining and artistically enriching. This is a "value-added" dimension of verbal beauty. God created the human spirit with a capacity and longing for the true, the good, and the beautiful. The wisdom literature of the Bible fulfills all three longings.

Repetition

Repetition is a standard rhetorical device, found in all forms of discourse and not limited to literature. One reason for the prevalence of repetition in literature is that it is an element of artistic form (along with such things as unity, variety, balance, contrast, and the like). At this level, repetition belongs with the beauty of expression that I discussed above. The famous poem on "a time for everything" (Eccl. 3:1–8) showcases its artistry by carefully arranging a series of fourteen parallel lines that repeat the following grammatical form: "a time to . . . and a time to . . ." (v. 2). The beatitudes of Jesus (Matt. 5:3–12) likewise use a repeated formula ("blessed are . . . for . . .") to create an artistic effect of beauty.

My concern here is the role of repetition in persuasion, and I will add the terms "argument" and "argumentation." One way to persuade someone is to conduct an argument, or follow a strategy of argumentation. It so happens that the wise men who gave us the wisdom literature of the Bible often operated on the premise that the way to prove a point is to keep repeating it until the reader or listener finally agrees that the statement is indeed true. I offer three examples.

The first is the poem at the beginning of Ecclesiastes (1:4–11) on the subject of the monotonous cycles of life that keep recurring and produce no discernible progress. This lament poem keeps adding to the list of examples until eight items have accumulated—four from nature (the cycle of generations, the sun, the wind, and water) and four from human experience (seeing, hearing, the absence of anything new, and the inability to remember and therefore being doomed to repeat the same cycle). A single principle (the cyclic nature of life) is repeated in different images. Here is a brief excerpt that shows the technique of repetition:

The sun rises, and the sun goes down,
    and hastens to the place where it rises.
The wind blows to the south
    and goes around to the north;
around and around goes the wind,
    and on its circuits the wind returns. (vv. 5–6)

As the sequence of examples unfolds and the cyclic quality of life is repeated, the point gradually settles in that life has a monotonous way of repeating itself without producing progression. The ancient Hebrew way of persuading us is to repeat a point until we agree.

My second example comes from Jesus' Sermon on the Mount. In Matthew 5:21–48, Jesus expounds on six religious practices, and in all instances he builds his argument around the formula "you have heard that it was said . . . but I say . . ." That repeated formula itself gradually convinces us that Jesus has come to reinterpret a commonly accepted rule inherited from either the Old Testament or Pharisaic additions to it. Within this general framework of repetition, the following (Matt. 5:23–25) is a typical instance of repeating the same idea:

> [23] So if you are offering your gift at the altar and there remember that your brother has something against you, [24] leave your gift there before the altar and go. First be reconciled to your brother, and then come and offer your gift. [25] Come to terms quickly with your accuser while you are going with him to court, lest your accuser hand you over to the judge, and the judge to the guard, and you be put in prison.

The core idea of quickly being reconciled is repeated in different words. The repetition represented by verse 25 drives the point home with greater persuasive force than verses 23–24 alone would.

In James 3:3–12, the author elaborates the point that the tongue is a small member that produces great harm when it is not controlled. James does not break the topic into subpoints but keeps repeating the core idea accompanied by analogies from nature. The following excerpt (vv. 5–6) illustrates this repetitive principle:

So also the tongue is a small member, yet it boasts of great things. How great a forest is set ablaze by such a small fire! And the tongue is a fire, a world of unrighteousness. The tongue is set among our members, staining the whole body, setting on fire the entire course of life, and set on fire by hell.

The effect of reading the passage is to be convinced that the tongue does, indeed, have the potential to be destructive.

The use of repetition as a way of conducting an argument has one main implication for interpretation: we need to avoid forcing a persuasive passage into the normal essay format of a thesis and multiple subpoints. In the type of passage I have been discussing, we find a common idea repeated, not a breaking of the main point into different subpoints.

Analogies to Nature

A hallmark of wisdom literature in the Bible is the use of analogies to nature. What this means is that the writer will take an excursion into the world of nature and then apply that data to a subject from the moral or spiritual life of people. As always with analogy, one area of life is used to shed light on another area. I offer three examples.

In Proverbs 6:27–29, the writer uses a standard wisdom literature technique: he first adduces two parallels to the real subject, and then, in the climactic position, he states his real point:

Can a man carry fire next to his chest
    and his clothes not be burned?
Or can one walk on hot coals
    and his feet not be scorched?
So is he who goes in to his neighbor's wife;
    none who touches her will go unpunished.

The persuasive strategy is as follows: if the first two items are demonstrably true, then the third one must also be true.

In the discourse against anxiety in the Sermon on the Mount (Matt. 6:25–34), Jesus repeatedly appeals to nature to support the idea that people can trust God's providence to provide for them. The following is an excerpt (vv. 26, 28–29):

> Look at the birds of the air: they neither sow nor reap nor gather into barns, and yet your heavenly Father feeds them. Are you not of more value than they? . . . And why are you anxious about clothing? Consider the lilies of the field, how they grow: they neither toil nor spin, yet I tell you, even Solomon in all his glory was not arrayed like one of these.

How can analogies to nature serve a persuasive function? They are irrefutable examples that we can all verify. If these things are incontrovertibly true in nature, they must also be true at a human level.

The following is a compact example from the epistle of James (1:11): "For the sun rises with its scorching heat and withers the grass; its flower falls, and its beauty perishes. So also will the rich man fade away in the midst of his pursuits."

The carryover value for interpretation is as follows. First, we need to experience the natural phenomena that the writer puts before us. We need to let the physical reality come alive. Then we need to carry over those meanings and associations to the actual subject of the statement. Additionally, if we realize that the analogies to nature function as a technique of persuasion, we can allow ourselves to be moved to assent and application. Finally, people universally have a love of nature. If a writer can tap into that longing, we are predisposed to respond favorably to what the writer says.

Rhetorical Questions

A rhetorical question is a question whose answer is apparent. This means that the question is not asked to secure information. What, then, is its purpose? The purpose is to move a reader or listener to assent, "Yes, this is in fact true." If we thus move someone to agree with us, we have persuaded that person to reach a conclusion or confirm a held position.

Rhetorical questions are sprinkled throughout the wisdom literature of the Bible. The following are three rhetorical questions from the book of Proverbs:

- "Why should you be intoxicated, my son, with a forbidden woman and embrace the bosom of an adulteress?" (5:20).
- "Does not he who keeps watch over your soul know it, and will he not repay man according to his work?" (24:12).
- "Does a crown endure to all generations?" (27:24).

The answers to these questions are self-evident. The wise man is not asking them because he does not know the answer but because he wants to engage the reader or listener in a process of agreeing. In answering each question, we have been persuaded anew of the truth of each one.

From the book of Ecclesiastes come the following examples. "Is there a thing of which it is said, / 'See, this is new'?" (1:10). "Do not all go to one place?" (6:6). "Who can tell man what will be after him under the sun?" (6:12). I have said that a rhetorical question engages the reader or listener in a process of agreement, but there is another angle as well. If the author can get us to agree with him in regard to the question he has asked, we are inclined to agree with what the author expresses elsewhere.

For my third batch, I dip into Jesus' Sermon on the Mount, but in doing so I want to say that many of Jesus' sayings throughout the Gospels are couched as rhetorical questions. Here are three examples from the Sermon on the Mount: "If salt has lost its taste, how shall its saltiness be restored?" (Matt. 5:13). "Which one of you, if his son asks him for bread, will give him a stone?" (Matt. 7:9). "Are grapes gathered from thornbushes, or figs from thistles?" (Matt. 7:16).

Positive and Negative Reinforcement

Wisdom literature is filled with human psychology. Many of the behavior traits and character types that we encounter are case studies in human personality. But there is also a more subtle level of psychology at work in wisdom literature. The proverbs frequently pair a command or observation with a statement of the result that accompanies the described situation or command. The following opposites become operative: reward and punishment, positive reinforcement and negative reinforcement, incentive and disincentive. The umbrella that covers all of these is motivation for conduct. We can also accurately think in terms of enlightened self-interest: many proverbs encourage us to act in our best interest by living virtuously.

The following are three examples of reward statements:

- "Commit your work to the Lord, / and your plans will be established" (Prov. 16:3).
- "But seek first the kingdom of God and his righteousness, and all these things will be added to you" (Matt. 6:33).
- "Humble yourselves before the Lord, and he will exalt you" (James 4:10).

Who would not desire to receive the promised rewards? They function as a motivation to obey the commands with which they are paired. This, in turn, can be regarded as a persuasive strategy.

The counterpart of positive reinforcement is a command or observation paired with a negative consequence. Here are three examples:

- "He who commits adultery lacks sense; / he who does it destroys himself" (Prov. 6:32).
- "Whoever troubles his own household will inherit the wind" (Prov. 11:29).
- "One who wanders from the way of good sense / will rest in the assembly of the dead" (Prov. 21:16).

The persuasive effect of these proverbs is to dissuade us from the action named in the first part of the proverb.

Even more common than the positive statement with reward and negative situation accompanied by a punishment is the two-line proverb in the form of antithetic parallelism:

- "Poverty and disgrace come to him who ignores instruction, / but whoever heeds reproof is honored" (Prov. 13:18).
- "Whoever trusts in his riches will fall, / but the righteous will flourish like a green leaf" (Prov. 11:28).
- "The plans of the diligent lead surely to abundance, / but everyone who is hasty comes only to poverty" (Prov. 21:5).

What all of the foregoing types demonstrate is that the proverbs of the Bible regularly offer positive reinforcement for good behavior and negative reinforcement for wrongdoing. That pattern, in turn, is part of the persuasive strategy of the wisdom writers.

Appeal to Human Experience

Thus far I have explored five forms of persuasion: verbal beauty, repetition, analogies to nature, rhetorical questions, and positive and negative reinforcement. These forms occur *regularly* in wisdom literature, but I need to guard against giving the impression that they occur *frequently*. I am never surprised when I come upon them, but when I compile a list of occurrences, I end up paging around a fair amount of time. By contrast, my final persuasive technique is omnipresent in wisdom literature.

Writers of proverbs and prose wisdom continuously take their subject matter from everyday life. Of course, this is true of literature generally: the subject of literature is human experience, and writers are gifted to observe the human scene and then record it. At several earlier points in this guide I have had occasion to say something about the rootedness of proverbs in real life. The new twist here is that the appeal to human experience is part of the persuasive strategy of the wisdom writers.

We can see this at work even in a freestanding proverb like the following one (Prov. 10:12): "Hatred stirs up strife, / but love covers all offenses." On what basis are we moved to agree with the wise man in this opinion? We ourselves have seen how much contentiousness is inflicted on people and institutions by people who hate them—doubly and triply so in a day of social media. We have equally seen or experienced how love toward people and institutions can counteract enmity that would otherwise erupt or lead offended people to forgive an offense. I would go so far as to say that we intuitively *know* that the proverb states the truth, based on our experiences of life.

The following meditative passage from Ecclesiastes (5:10–12) illustrates the same persuasive strategy in prose. The subject of the passage can be labeled "the case against money." With that as the governing motif, the author then spins out a series of variations on the central theme. The passage is as follows:

> He who loves money will not be satisfied with money, nor he who loves wealth with his income; this also is vanity. When goods increase, they increase who eat them, and what advantage has their owner but to see them with his eyes? Sweet is the sleep of a laborer, whether he eats little or much, but the full stomach of the rich will not let him sleep.

In sequence, the arguments against devoting one's life to making money are as follows: money does not satisfy permanently and at the deepest level and therefore leads to constant dissatisfaction; the only advantage of having lots of possessions is that it gives a person more to look at (a sarcastic putdown); endless anxieties attend wealth.

I remind my readers that what this collection of proverbs requires us to do is reflect on our own experiences of the situations that are described and our observations of others. Of course, this requires pondering on our part, as we place individual proverbs into a real-life context. But reading slowly and thoughtfully and analytically goes with the territory of mastering wisdom literature. As we do this required spadework, we will confirm the accuracy of each proverb. The appeal is to human experience.

How does this become a tactic of persuasion? It begins with an acknowledgment that the author "got it right" at the experiential level. For example, we have experienced and observed how money does not satisfy, how a big house gradually loses its luster, and how worried people with money and many possessions are. Then, perhaps at a subconscious level, we gravitate toward the position that it would be foolish for us to chase after money and possessions. Or we might very consciously decide, in the face of the evidence, not to live for wealth.

LEARNING BY DOING

I have saved the application for the end of the chapter because the piecemeal application would have been too easy and a little artificial. So I offer the following long passage as one that will allow you to apply many (but not all) of the persuasive strategies the chapter has covered. If you discern additional ones, that is entirely appropriate. The passage is James 2:14–26:

What good is it, my brothers, if someone says he has faith but does not have works? Can that faith save him? If a brother or sister is poorly clothed and lacking in daily food, and one of you says to them, "Go in peace, be warmed and filled," without giving them the things needed for the body, what good is that? So also faith by itself, if it does not have works, is dead.

But someone will say, "You have faith and I have works." Show me your faith apart from your works, and I will show you my faith by my works. You believe that God is one; you do well. Even the demons believe—and shudder! Do you want to be shown, you foolish person, that faith apart from works is useless? Was not Abraham our father justified by works when he offered up his son Isaac on the altar? You see that faith was active along with his works, and faith was completed by his works; and the Scripture was fulfilled that says, "Abraham believed God, and it was counted to him as righteousness"—and he was called a friend of God. You see that a person is justified by works and not by faith alone. And in the same way was not also Rahab the prostitute justified by works when she received the messengers and sent them out by another way? For as the body apart from the spirit is dead, so also faith apart from works is dead.

If you wish to supplement that passage and apply a greater range of what this chapter has covered, Jesus' discourse against anxiety (Matt. 6:25–34) is a good text to choose.